Elements in Language Teaching
edited by
Heath Rose
University of Oxford
Jim McKinley
University College London

TEACHING SECOND LANGUAGE ACADEMIC WRITING

Christine M. Tardy
University of Arizona

Shaftesbury Road, Cambridge CB2 8EA, United Kingdom

One Liberty Plaza, 20th Floor, New York, NY 10006, USA

477 Williamstown Road, Port Melbourne, VIC 3207, Australia

314–321, 3rd Floor, Plot 3, Splendor Forum, Jasola District Centre, New Delhi – 110025, India

103 Penang Road, #05-06/07, Visioncrest Commercial, Singapore 238467

Cambridge University Press is part of Cambridge University Press & Assessment, a department of the University of Cambridge.

We share the University's mission to contribute to society through the pursuit of education, learning and research at the highest international levels of excellence.

www.cambridge.org
Information on this title: www.cambridge.org/9781009638333

DOI: 10.1017/9781009638326

© Christine M. Tardy 2025

This publication is in copyright. Subject to statutory exception and to the provisions of relevant collective licensing agreements, no reproduction of any part may take place without the written permission of Cambridge University Press & Assessment.

When citing this work, please include a reference to the DOI 10.1017/9781009638326

First published 2025

A catalogue record for this publication is available from the British Library

ISBN 978-1-009-63833-3 Hardback
ISBN 978-1-009-63831-9 Paperback
ISSN 2632-4415 (online)
ISSN 2632-4407 (print)

Cambridge University Press & Assessment has no responsibility for the persistence or accuracy of URLs for external or third-party internet websites referred to in this publication and does not guarantee that any content on such websites is, or will remain, accurate or appropriate.

Teaching Second Language Academic Writing

Elements in Language Teaching

DOI: 10.1017/9781009638326
First published online: February 2025

Christine M. Tardy
University of Arizona

Author for correspondence: Christine M. Tardy, ctardy@arizona.edu

Abstract: This Element offers readers an overview of the theory, research, and practice of teaching academic writing to second language/multilingual (L2) students. The Element begins with a discussion of contextual features and some of the most common settings in which L2AW is taught. The Element then defines and shares examples of several concepts, pedagogical approaches, and teaching practices that are particularly relevant to L2AW instruction. Reflective questions guide readers to consider how these aspects of L2AW might be carried out within their own educational settings. Finally, the Element considers the rapid changes in technology and their influences on texts and academic writing.

Keywords: L2 writing, multilingual writing, academic writing, writing instruction, language teaching

© Christine M. Tardy 2025

ISBNs: 9781009638333 (HB), 9781009638319 (PB), 9781009638326 (OC)
ISSNs: 2632-4415 (online), 2632-4407 (print)

Contents

1 Introduction	1
2 Contexts of Teaching L2AW	3
3 Important Concepts for Teaching L2 Academic Writing	15
4 Approaches In Teaching L2 Academic Writing	30
5 Teaching Practices in L2AW	41
6 Future Directions of Academic Writing	57
References	62

1 Introduction

Academic knowledge is largely passed down through written texts, and academic contexts are partly characterized by their heavy reliance on the written word. Knowledge is communicated to students often in the form of publications like textbooks, research articles, and scholarly books. Instruction is often supplemented by lecture notes, presentation slides, worksheets and handouts, written (online) discussions, and assignment instructions. Students also do their own share of academic writing. Students' knowledge of course content, for example, is often assessed through writing, in the form of written exercises, lab reports, papers, and essay exams. As students begin contributing to academic knowledge, they compose research posters, proposals, reports, and theses.

A large number of students worldwide compose academic writing in a language that is not their first, primary, or dominant language. In many settings, for instance, students' education is delivered in a second or additional language (L2). The most prominent such example is English medium instruction (EMI), "the use of the English language to teach academic subjects (other than English itself) in countries or jurisdictions where the first language of the majority population is not English" (Macaro et al., 2018, p. 37). Though exact numbers are elusive, EMI already has a firm foothold in Europe, Asia, and the Middle East, while it appears to be in earlier stages of expansion in Latin America and Africa (Lasagabaster, 2022). In addition to EMI, in which students are typically learning in another language "at home," there are around 6.4 million "internationally mobile students" in higher education, studying at universities abroad (UNESCO UIS, 2024). This population includes many students who are studying in an L2; the United States and the United Kingdom are the most popular destinations, but Germany, France, Türkiye, China, South Korea, and Russia also host large numbers of international students (Migration Data Portal, n.d.). In sum, L2AW occurs all over the world and in numerous languages.

1.1 What Is Second Language Writing?

Second language writing is a field of study that examines writing and the teaching and learning of writing in an additional language. The field encompasses various educational, workplace, and community contexts, and includes writing in *any* additional language, though English as an additional language (EAL) has tended to dominate the scholarship. Second language writing is an interdisciplinary field, which draws on research traditions and pedagogical practices primarily from applied linguistics and rhetoric and composition (Matsuda, 1999; Silva & Leki, 2004), and in different contexts it may draw on other relevant fields like education and anthropology. The term *second language writing* is also used to describe courses and instruction for second language (multilingual) writers as well as the texts created by these writers.

Second language writing is not an uncontested label. "Second language" is generally used to refer to a second, third, or other additional language—that is, any language beyond one's first or dominant language. Of course, many "second language" writers may actually be more comfortable writing in their additional language than their first language. There are also good arguments for replacing "second language" with "multilingual" writers for a more asset-based orientation. At the same time, second language writing is a more familiar term in many language teaching contexts, and it is also the label used in numerous publications (including the flagship *Journal of Second Language Writing*) and scholarly and pedagogical settings. In this Element, I use L2 as shorthand for the full set of labels that might apply to an additional or nondominant language. Therefore, an "L2 writer" can be considered a multilingual writer, additional language writer, second language writer, translingual writer, and so on.

1.2 The Scope and Aims of This Element

There are many excellent publications that provide broad surveys of L2 writing (Ferris & Hedgcock, 2023; Hyland, 2019; Manchón & Matsuda, 2016; Leki, Cumming, & Silva, 2010). This Cambridge Element is not a substitute for those comprehensive overviews of the field or its research and pedagogical practices. Instead, here I focus more narrowly on one particular sub-area: teaching L2 academic writing, or, for sake of ease, L2AW. Academic writing here refers to written texts that are used for the pursuit of teaching and learning, knowledge dissemination, and knowledge construction. Though academic writing occurs in K–12 education, this Element focuses primarily on the more advanced academic writing found in higher education.

A fairly large body of research and teaching resources now exist to support L2AW instruction, making it impossible to incorporate all of these insights here. Instead, my goal is more modest: to introduce practitioners to some of the key concepts, research insights, and pedagogical practices in L2AW. Therefore, this Element is not a guidebook of how to teach L2AW but instead lays the groundwork for current and future teachers to develop their own "small-t theories" about such instruction. Atkinson (2010) describes such theories as "the opposite of Theory with a big T . . . [similar to] the postmodernist idea of *petits récits*—theories that engage with particular, local situations" (p. 8). He goes on to say that

Teaching Second Language Academic Writing 3

> Theory with a small t presents no already-made, all-knowing prescription for what is wrong with the world and how to fix it. Rather, it offers *small* tools that will help people build their *own* understanding (or not—there is no sense in which one *must* use these tools) of social situations and power structures which will be relevant and useful in their own situations, including how to change them. (pp. 11–12)

Our small-t theories are individual, critical, and constantly developing as we read, teach, learn, and discuss our experiences in offices, classrooms, webinars, social media, and over tea. Small-t theories are a kind of reflective practice that help us make sense of our experiences and give us tools to ask why we do what we do, how our practice affects others, and how we might do otherwise. The goal of this Element is to offer a contribution to readers' own small-t theories about L2AW instruction.

1.3 How to Use This Element

This Element is organized around the assumption that all teaching and learning is deeply contextual. As a result, there is no one way to teach or a single set of strategies that can be used with success in every classroom, with every learner, or by every teacher. The goal for teachers, instead, should be to establish a strong understanding of the local elements that shape their educational setting and of key concepts, principles, and practices of learning and teaching.

First, in Section 2, we'll explore the various contextual features that can have a significant impact on educational choices in L2AW. A framework guides readers through these features as a way to consider how they might impact a L2AW classroom. This section also discusses some of the more common settings of L2AW and their unique characteristics. Following this discussion, the next three sections outline some of the most important concepts (Section 3), pedagogical approaches (Section 4), and pedagogical practices (Section 5) in L2AW. Together, these sections offer readers a toolkit for making pedagogical decisions in their own settings. Finally, the Element ends in Section 6 with a consideration of how rapid changes in technology are influencing L2AW and its instruction.

2 Contexts of Teaching L2AW

General principles of teaching L2AW do exist, and we will explore many of those in later sections. At the same time, teachers quickly learn that the decisions made on a daily basis—in each class period, and indeed with each group of students—do not occur in a vacuum. Rather, teachers are constantly assessing what is appropriate *in this particular situation* and acting accordingly. For example, the choice of assignments, the approaches to assessment, and the kinds of activities should all take into account aspects of the local pedagogical setting. This section outlines some of the important contextual considerations that shape L2AW instruction, and it provides an overview of the most common settings in which L2AW is taught. The contextual features discussed can serve as a kind of heuristic or "thinking framework" for teachers as they plan and reflect on their own instruction.

2.1 Important Features of L2AW Settings

L2AW instructional settings vary widely across several contextual levels, such as geographical location, institution type, program type, population, and local language policies and ideologies. Effective instruction, as a result, must adapt to local needs and circumstances, accounting for such features in instructional decisions from course design to classroom activities to feedback and assessment practices.

Figure 1 depicts some of the important contextual features for teachers to consider in planning and teaching courses: languages and genres, language attitudes and ideologies, language policies, educational practices, and writers. These features are relevant at multiple contextual levels, from the broad geographical context of the instruction, to the institution, program, and specific classroom. Although no framework can fully do justice to a complex ecology, Figure 1 offers a basic map for understanding an instructional context. The subsections that follow elaborate on the contextual features represented in the figure.

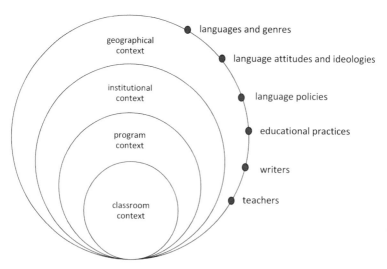

Figure 1 A heuristic for identifying important features of an instructional context.

2.1.1 Languages and Genres

One of the first considerations in L2AW instruction is the kinds of communication that occur in the particular setting and that are important for the student writers. For example, L2AW teachers need to know the languages that are used in the target setting(s) and the functions they carry out. In academic writing, functions become indexed largely through *genres*. Genre is described in more detail in Section 3, but in simple terms, it refers to conventionalized (written and multimodal) practices used to carry out common functions or actions within social communities. Some academic writing genres include research articles, grant proposals, case study reports, and scientific posters. The genres that are important for students vary across educational contexts. For example, graduate students in an engineering program need to use very different genres from undergraduate students in a general university writing course.

Using the framework in Figure 1, a teacher can consider languages and genres at various contextual levels that are relevant to their teaching situation. At the geographical level, it is useful to understand which languages are prominent in the region(s) and what those languages are used for. Kachru (1986) referred to this latter issue as *functional allocation*, describing the functions that different languages take on within a society. For instance, within a multilingual society, people may use one language in religious services, another language for most interpersonal communication, and another language for education. This functional allocation of languages to carry out different activities in our lives also impacts which genres are used in different languages. For example, in some contexts, English is the language of education, so students may be most accustomed to using academic genres in English even if it is their additional language.

Institutional settings often use a narrower range of languages and genres compared to the wider geographic setting, so teachers will also want to consider this contextual level. An international school may use languages and genres that are rarely found outside of the school. In other settings, however, an institution's languages of use may be identical to those common in the local geography. Institutionally, some genres may be produced in multiple languages, while others may only ever use one language.

Within institutions, writing and language instruction is often directed by programs, and these units typically have a significant impact on instruction. Language centers, writing programs, or postgraduate communication programs can also use different languages and genres than are used in the larger institution. An English for Academic Purposes (EAP) program at a Japanese university, for instance, will emphasize the use of English, though other courses and extracurricular events at the university may primarily use Japanese.

Finally, even within a program, L2AW teachers will want to learn about the languages and genres that are relevant for the students in their classroom: Which genres are most motivating to these students? Which are most important? Do they write these genres in multiple languages or just in one language? How are they similar and different? Further, in some L2AW classes, students may share the same first language, while other classrooms may encompass students from diverse language backgrounds. Students within a classroom can also have different relationships to the L2, regardless of proficiency; for example, an L2 Arabic classroom in Canada or the UK is very likely to include both students for whom Arabic is a heritage language and those who have no home relationship to the language.

2.1.2 Language Attitudes and Ideologies

Identifying the prominent languages and genres is only the first step in gaining a rich understanding of an L2AW context. Research shows that language attitudes and ideologies can also impact learning and should therefore inform instructional decisions (McGroarty, 2010). The two concepts can be hard to tease apart, but King (2000) offers a useful distinction: Language attitudes are "directed towards a specific object," while ideologies "refer to a broader system of beliefs, norms, or values" (p. 168).

At the geographical level, dominant attitudes toward the L2 can affect practical issues for L2AW, such as funding, resources, and teacher availability, as well as issues like motivation or perceptions of the language's value or importance. Language attitudes and ideologies are impacted by politics, international relations, and current events as well. To share a personal example, I have seen student enrollment in my son's dual-language Mandarin-English program in elementary school dwindle as relations between the United States and China have deteriorated. The complex history and role of English around the world presents another example: In many countries, English has become a common language for education because of a perception that English is important for global participation and perhaps even for personal financial and social success (Lasagabaster, 2022). At the same time, English is often (rightly) associated with colonialism and empire, as well as capitalist and neoliberal ideologies. There is also the further complication that different language varieties may be more or less valued in a geographical setting—and ideologies that value standard language varieties, monolingualism, or multilingualism also impact instructional settings (Wiley & Lukes, 1996). Geographical settings are heterogeneous spaces, so attitudes and ideologies are likely to be multiple and conflicting rather than unitary.

Teaching Second Language Academic Writing

At the institutional and program levels of L2AW instruction, language attitudes and ideologies may align or conflict with the wider social context. For example, a dual-language school in which students build literacy in two languages can be located within a geographical region where monolingualism dominates. The language ideologies and attitudes in a program can also differ from the larger institution. It is not unusual, for instance, for language and writing programs to value multilingualism or diverse language varieties more highly than their institutional homes.

Institutions, programs, and classrooms can hold complicated attitudes not just toward the L2 and its varieties but also toward *writing*. For example, even institutions and programs that value linguistic diversity may teach or assess academic writing in ways that suppress that diversity (Horner & Trimbur, 2002). A given classroom is also likely to encompass a range of language ideologies and attitudes, from both the students' and teachers' perspectives. Similarly, teachers who value linguistic diversity may find themselves still adopting and reinforcing more restrictive language practices. L2AW teachers will do well to understand the complex ways in which language attitudes and ideologies impact their institutions, programs, and individual classrooms.

2.1.3 Language Policies

For many people, language policies call to mind rules or regulations that stipulate or restrict language use in a particular setting. In applied linguistics, following Spolsky (2004), language policy is often considered to be made up of three components: language practices (i.e., people's actual choices and uses of particular languages or varieties), language beliefs or ideologies, and actual interventions or management intended to influence language practice. These components are also interrelated and can shape one another. For instance, management policies that promote monolingualism may also normalize monolingual or standard language ideology and thus lead to negative attitudes towards linguistic diversity.

At the geographic level, we can look to national language policies, which exert a powerful influence on education. Some countries, for example, have promoted the use of additional languages, with a focus on language instruction or medium of instruction in schools. When a language becomes common or required in the educational system, it will be used for more purposes, expanding the genres it is used to carry out as well as its perceived importance in society. At the same time, language policies may ignore, actively promote, or actively suppress the use of nondominant languages, such as the languages used by indigenous communities, ethnically marginalized communities, and immigrants and refugees.

We can also consider language policy at the level of institutions and programs, both of which influence L2AW instruction. Higher education institutions, for instance, may require a certain number of foreign language courses (or demonstrated proficiency) for graduation, or students may need to demonstrate proficiency in the language of instruction for admission. An institution's language-related policies may lead to the development of courses and other services (such as tutoring centers) to support students in meeting these requirements. Even when no explicit language policies exist, institutional and program practices create *de facto* policies—that is, unstated practices that become normalized and routinely followed (Shohamy, 2006). The assumed use of English for academic coursework in most US institutions, for instance, creates a *de facto* policy of English Only.

L2AW program and classroom language policies may also be overtly articulated (e.g., a program's or teacher's policies toward multilingual use in the classroom) or just reinforced through practice. In settings where writing or language programs lack overt policies about language use, an institution's or region's dominant policies (formal or de facto) will likely hold sway. In such cases, faculty and student dialogue can help to learn more about the community's values and desires for L2AW instruction; such conversations can eventually lead to the ground-up articulation of program visions or goals related to language policies (Tardy, 2011).

Within their own L2AW classroom contexts, teachers may construct, work within, resist, or challenge language policies. Discussing with students how policies and ideologies shape their goals for academic writing (see, for example, Swales, 1997) can help students recognize the social and political forces that influence language and writing. Without such explicit attention, normative language policies are likely to dominate in many settings.

2.1.4 Educational Practices

Educational practices in L2AW—ranging from course design to classroom activities to assessment (see Section 5)—can vary greatly within national contexts, institutions, programs, and classrooms. Geographic settings are always heterogeneous in educational practices, but there may be widely shared practices due to language policies, ideologies, and so on. For example, in some regions, education is very test-driven; in L2AW instruction, this practice can contribute to an emphasis on timed writing, formulaic text types, and over-attention to grammatical accuracy. Geographical areas can also share expectations about typical roles for teachers and students. Do teachers typically lecture and distribute information with students? Do students ask questions or contribute to knowledge construction in the classroom? How common are practices like peer review, collaborative writing, or class discussion?

Teaching Second Language Academic Writing 9

Variations in educational practices are also evident at the institutional level. Secondary schools and universities, for instance, often differ in how academic writing is taught and assessed and which genres are emphasized. Even within an institution, L2AW instructional practices can vary across programs. Atkinson and Ramanathan (1995), for example, studied the instruction in a university's intensive English (preparatory) program and the same university's undergraduate writing program and found important distinctions in the types of writing that were taught and valued. Institutions and programs may also vary in their access to and uses of technology, which impact writing instruction. Do students have access to computers within or outside of the classroom? What kinds of apps are commonly used, discouraged, or banned within the institution, program, or classroom? Many writing and language programs may also have shared assessment practices, such as recommended rubrics, program-wide portfolio requirements, or program exit exams. Program learning outcomes can also exert significant influence on course design and instruction, as students may need to demonstrate achievement of such outcomes through summative assessment measures.

At the classroom level, educational practices may be tightly controlled by program guidelines, or L2AW teachers may be highly autonomous, implementing their own approaches to course design and instruction. The modality of instruction is also an important consideration today, with an increase in online teaching. Today's L2AW classrooms may be taught in person, in a synchronous online environment, through asynchronous instruction in a learning management system, or even in a hybrid environment. Each of these modalities influences a teacher's pedagogical choices.

2.1.5 Writers

Within this complex ecology, we cannot forget about the student-writers themselves. L2 academic writers make up a diverse group, with many people using their additional language(s) to write in academic settings. The label of "L2 writer" (or L2 academic writer) is merely shorthand for a much more complex constellation of people, and the limitations of that label are also important for teachers to recognize. Some "L2 writers" have learned their additional language through instruction, while others may have learned it through immersion after moving to a new country or city (Valdés, 1992); some may be new learners and others may have been using their L2 their whole lives. Further, many advanced academic writers are actually more comfortable writing in their additional language than in their home language or mother tongue, depending on which language they primarily use for academic purposes. Therefore, to understand a student population of "L2 academic writers," we must think along several population levels, from broad geographic populations to populations within our institutions, programs, and courses.

Within an institutional setting, teachers may find that writers share some relevant characteristics. For instance, students enrolled at an engineering and science school may have different writing goals, ways of learning, and prior written genre experiences than students enrolled at a fine arts institution. Institutional, program, and classroom populations can also differ in socioeconomic status, linguistic backgrounds, career goals, or educational preparation. Therefore, gathering more insight about students through surveys, writing prompts, and classroom discussions will greatly benefit L2AW teachers. Teachers should also take into account how students view themselves, both as writers and (biliterate) language users (e.g., Ortmeier-Hooper, 2008; Séror & Gentil, 2020).

As we strive to understand our students as complex beings with dynamic and even conflicting identities, teachers may find the lens of intersectionality to be particularly useful. An intersectionality framework encourages "understanding power relations at the intersection of language and other social categories across different domains of power" (Kayı-Aydar, 2023, p. 5). In other words, people are never just a unitary identity—for example, L2 writer or international student or Chinese or female or queer. Adopting an openness to viewing students as complex and ever-changing individuals helps teachers not just to avoid stereo-typing students but also to consider "how an individual's social standing in the material world intersects or interacts with other identity markers in shaping an individual's cultural and societal experiences" (Kayı-Aydar, 2023, p. 8). This lens can also help L2AW teachers reflect on how our pedagogical choices and practices position our students, what opportunities those practices offer students for growth, and what opportunities they may inadvertently foreclose.

2.1.6 Teachers

As teachers, we are also a part of the educational ecologies in which we plan classes, prepare materials, and assess students. A final step of taking a critical lens to the contexts of L2AW therefore involves looking inward at what we ourselves bring to the context.

We may consider, for example, our own geographical backgrounds. Where were we educated and what biases or assumptions about education might we hold based on that background? How have our experiences, perhaps teaching or learning in different contexts, shaped how we tend to teach or what we value in the classroom? How does our knowledge of or familiarity with the linguistic and cultural backgrounds of our students impact what we (can) do in the classroom?

At an institutional and program level, teachers' practices are further shaped by workload, salary, job security, teacher autonomy, and collegiality. A teacher who holds jobs at multiple institutions, with different curricula and over 150 students, will not have a great deal of time to develop their own teaching materials or to provide substantial feedback on student drafts in comparison with a teacher who holds a full-time position and teaches 80 students in total. Further, class size, classroom facilities, time of day, and even safety of the environment all impact the choices we make as L2AW teachers.

Teachers should also critically question their role in the classroom. In a profession which often reinforces racial hierarchies, L2AW teachers should reflect on how their own national origin, race, gender, ethnicity, sexual orientation, visible disabilities, and so on position us within a classroom. Academic writing is undeniably implicated in creating and maintaining systems of power in educational settings and often beyond. L2AW teachers should hold a critical awareness of this imbalance and regularly step back to consider how what we do in the classroom might serve to reproduce such structures and where we might act differently if and when we can.

2.2 Common Settings of L2AW Instruction

The contextual ecology described in Section 2.1 is intended to provide a broad schema for L2AW teachers in considering instructional choices. This section describes some of the more common settings of L2AW instruction, highlighting their important characteristics.

2.2.1 Pre-University Language Preparation Programs

Many universities offer language preparation courses for students who have not yet fulfilled language proficiency requirements for enrollment. These courses are often part of an intensive English program (IEP) or language center in which students take multiple language courses in an intensive language curriculum; such programs exist in English-dominant countries as well as in countries where English is not the dominant language but may be a university's medium of instruction. Language preparation programs often serve both undergraduate and graduate students, though usually in separate courses. Programs can differ in the extent to which writing is taught as a discrete skill or is integrated with reading, listening, and/or speaking instruction.

Some language preparation programs also offer "pathway" programs for students who are provisionally admitted to the university and/or have nearly reached language proficiency requirements. Pathway programs come in different configurations but often include so-called sheltered university classes, in which pathway students form their own class section, sometimes with additional language support. Pathway programs may include writing courses as well as other courses that include writing and may have some writing instruction.

Pre-university L2AW instruction may teach more general writing types (e.g., argumentative, analytic, narrative) because of the heterogeneous population of students in a course. Shared curricula and assessment are often common in these programs, as well.

2.2.2 Early Undergraduate Education

One very common setting of L2AW instruction is early undergraduate education. In many countries, L2 writing instruction at this level is often integrated within broader English for academic purposes (EAP) courses. Writing instruction may be the focus of specific writing courses, or it may be part of more integrated skills courses. In many EAP programs, students take multiple courses in a sequenced manner, allowing students to gradually build complex academic literacy practices related to writing from sources, development of ideas, and writing flexibly across rhetorical situations. Other programs may be limited to single courses in which teachers must prioritize areas of instruction.

In the United States, L2AW instruction in early undergraduate education typically falls within university writing programs and courses labeled as first year writing (FYW), first year composition, or freshman composition (here I use the abbreviation FYW). FYW programs often serve monolingual and multilingual students, with multilingual students including domestic and international (visa-holding) students. These populations may be taught in the same classrooms, separated by policy into "mainstream" and "L2" sections, or be given choices in which sections they enroll in (Tardy & Miller-Cochran, 2018). At some institutions, international L2 writers are taught through a separate program, further illustrating the ways that institutional policies and structures impact L2AW. Language instruction is generally given less attention in FYW programs (Matsuda, 2012), but it may take on a more prominent role in programs or courses designed specifically for L2 writers.

Many early undergraduate writing classes include students from across the disciplines in one class. Such cross-disciplinary courses emphasize more generalizable aspects of writing, such as rhetorical awareness and flexibility, critical thinking, and strategies for composing and revising.

2.2.3 Undergraduate Writing in the Disciplines

When undergraduate writing instruction groups students by discipline, classroom instruction may place more emphasis on familiarizing students with the genres and discourses of their field. Such instruction would fall under the label of English for specific academic purposes, in contrast to English for general academic purposes (Charles, 2012; Hyland, 2016).

Disciplinary writing can be taught in the early or upper levels of undergraduate education. For instance, disciplinary areas sometimes offer courses specifically focused on writing instruction, such as business writing, professional writing, legal writing, literary analysis, or writing for science courses. In these cases, instructors often have expertise in writing instruction while also being familiar with the disciplinary genres and their unique features. Disciplinary writing can also be taught within the context of a disciplinary content course, in which students write major projects and receive some writing instruction support (Bazerman et al., 2005). In this latter case, instructors are more likely to be disciplinary experts who have some training in writing instruction.

2.2.4 Postgraduate L2AW and Writing for Publication

L2AW instruction at the postgraduate level—that is, students in master's or doctoral degree or professional programs—tends to be highly specific in the genres taught, though students from different disciplinary areas (science and engineering, humanities, social sciences, fine arts) may be grouped together in instruction. Writing courses in this context generally emphasize the genres that are needed for success in graduate school (especially theses and dissertations) and at the early stages of academic scholarship (e.g., research articles, conference posters, book reviews, and grant proposals).

Postgraduate writing courses often teach writing for publication, especially given the increasing demands in many countries to publish before graduating. Additionally, writing for publication courses may also include junior scholars, or even senior scholars who desire support in publishing in their nondominant language (see, for example, Corcoran, 2017). L2AW instruction at this level is not limited to courses; it may also include tutoring, workshops, boot camps or writing retreats, and writing groups (Caplan & Cox, 2016).

2.3 Learning about Your L2AW Context

This discussion of contextual considerations for teachers is rather detailed—and perhaps a bit overwhelming! How can a teacher possibly learn *everything* about a context and the individuals in any given class? For better or worse, we will

14 *Language Teaching*

never be able to fully understand the ecological environments in which we teach. Instead, the goal of the framework discussed here is to offer starting points for learning about our contexts and students.

This learning process should be ongoing and in many ways resembles a needs analysis (Bocanegra-Valle, 2016). Learning about a geographical region, for example, may mean understanding policies related to language, education, and even immigration, as well as social structures and ideologies that position students in relation to language, socioeconomic class, race, ethnicity, and other areas. Building such local knowledge involves being aware of legislation, political discussions, educational policies, and community conversations. Learning about an institutional or program context similarly means taking an explicit eye toward local policies and practices and how they impact learning and teaching. Such contexts are constantly evolving, so it is important for programs to regularly gather information about students and teachers and to frequently revisit their goals, values, and language-related policies. At the classroom level, teachers have the most direct opportunity to learn about their individual students. Student surveys, in-class discussions, writing assignments about their literacy histories and beliefs can all help teachers gain more insight into their students.

Most importantly, though, the ecological components of L2AW described in this section are intended to provide points of reflection for future and current teachers. By taking moments to break down the numerous elements of a teaching context, we can better evaluate a situation and ask questions that can lead to informed classroom choices.

Reflection

1. Using the components in Figure 1, create a table, list, drawing, or other visual that outlines some of the most important features of your current or desired instructional setting for L2 academic writing.

2. Write one or two paragraphs discussing how these features might impact aspects of your instruction, including, for example: learning outcomes or course goals, the types of genres you might teach, the types of classroom activities you might use, how you might assess student work, how you might approach language diversity (and adherence to particular norms or varieties of the language).

3. Identify a few tools or methods you could use to gather more, ongoing, and/or updated information about your teaching contexts and students.

3 Important Concepts for Teaching L2 Academic Writing

L2AW instruction involves teaching a second language, teaching writing, and teaching academic literacy—all in an integrated way. It is insufficient for teachers to understand language, writing, *or* academic practices and contexts; instead, they must understand all of these areas and their interaction, along with many related concepts. A tall order indeed. This section outlines some of the most important concepts that can inform the teaching of L2AW, beginning with the very broad concept of language. Readers will notice that the concepts in this section build upon each other and intertwine increasingly as they progress through this section. Overall, the section aims to provide a starting point for understanding concepts that should impact how we think about L2AW and its development.

3.1 Language

As Hyland (2007) has aptly stated, "Teachers of writing clearly need to be teachers of language, as it is an ability to exercise appropriate linguistic choices in the ways they treat and organise their topics for particular readers which helps students to give their ideas authority" (p. 151). Perhaps somewhat surprisingly, however, the role of language in writing instruction is often overlooked or overshadowed by the many aspects of writing instruction.

Defining language is not a straightforward task. A more traditional grammar-based approach views language as the words and grammatical structures that are used as signs for meaning making. In academic writing research, there is a strong tradition for researching the linguistic choices commonly made in academic settings. Academic language, for example, has been shown to differ from conversation in its complexity, with conversation making more use of subordinate clauses (e.g., ***When you get there***, *call me*) but academic writing featuring a higher frequency of complex noun phrases (e.g., ***A more traditional grammar-based approach*** *views language as . . .*) (Biber et al., 2011). A sizable body of research has also more specifically explored the linguistic features typical of L2 writers' texts, often in comparison with texts by monolingual writers (e.g., Eckstein & Ferris, 2018; Staples & Reppen, 2016). This comparative approach may be less dominant today, partly due to an increased recognition that variation among writers is just as likely to be related to their relative experience or expertise than to their linguistic background (Swales, 2004). Language-based studies have also examined L2 writers' texts in their own right, for example, looking at linguistic features of writers using English as a Lingua Franca (ELF) or varieties of World Englishes (Hynninen & Kuteeva, 2017; Rozycki & Johnson, 2013).

This kind of research can help teachers and students identify aspects of language that may impact how their texts are received by intended audiences or how language choices specifically align with the goals of a text and even the values of a community of users. A simple example to illustrate this relationship between language choices and audience can be found in an exercise in Swales and Feak's (2020) textbook *Academic Writing for Graduate Students*, in which students consider which evaluative adjectives are most common in research writing across different disciplines. (They learn, for instance, that *elegant* is popular in physics, *rigorous* in social sciences, and *original* in humanities.)

Polio (2019) has argued that, in many SLW classrooms, language is given insufficient attention and that such instruction should "expand [students'] linguistic resources so that they have a larger arsenal of vocabulary, grammar, and chunks of language as well as the knowledge to decide among linguistic choices to communicate in a pragmatically appropriate way" (p. 1). One approach that can help students reach this goal is explicit language instruction that emphasizes the effects of different language choices (Caplan, 2022). This functional approach is tied to a broader theory of language known as Systemic Functional Linguistics (SFL). In a functional approach, language instruction in academic writing strives to familiarize students with how lexical and grammatical choices carry meaning and function and to help students develop "independent control of a broadening linguistic repertoire" (Caplan, 2022, p. 468). For example, when teaching academic summary writing, teachers may draw students' attention to the common use of reporting verbs (*This study found that . . .; Caplan argues that . . .*). Students can compare summaries with and without reporting verbs to explore how they can alter the meaning or emphasis of a text; they can further analyze what kinds of verbs are commonly used (e.g., *find, suggest, explore*) and which are relatively uncommon (e.g., *say, get*).

Furthermore, language can also be understood to be much more than a grammatical system. As a social semiotic (Halliday, 1978), language is also considered a resource for communicating within social contexts. In fact, its variation across settings and purposes makes this additional *social* dimension of language quite visible. Atkinson (2002) adopts a sociocognitive perspective to describe language as "an abundantly rich resource for getting on in the world—for performing social action. Language is intricately but dynamically interwoven with humans' other means of ecological adaptation and activity" (p. 536). Learning a second language, in this view, involves much more than developing control over a set of linguistic features.

Language has also been at the heart of many tensions in scholarly discussions of teaching academic writing. Today, many researchers and teachers recognize that linguistic diversity is a natural part of language use and one that should be

Teaching Second Language Academic Writing

valued rather than erased. Yet, in academic writing, valuing linguistic diversity is often at odds with practices like classroom evaluation, standardized testing, and editorial gatekeeping, all of which tend to push writers toward conformity rather than diversity. L2AW teachers can benefit from articulating their own understanding of what language is and what its role(s) in L2AW instruction can and should be.

3.2 Multilingualism and Multicompetence

Many aspects of teaching and learning academic writing are similar for monolingual and multilingual writers. In all cases, writers need to learn how to control a written linguistic and rhetorical repertoire in ways that will be effective in an academic setting. Yet, there are also distinctions. As an aside, though monolingualism and multilingualism are typically presented as dichotomies, like many concepts, they may be better conceived of as dynamic continua, as an individual's multilingual repertoires may shift and be more or less valued in different sociolinguistic contexts (Blommaert et al., 2005). Take, for instance, a multilingual user of Tagalog and English who grew up in Chicago and is a university student. While that student may feel equally comfortable in Tagalog and English in family settings, they may have a very limited repertoire of academic Tagalog due to years of schooling in English only.

Multilingualism, broadly, refers to the use of two or more languages by individuals, groups, or societies (Cenoz, 2013). Therefore, we can refer to a student, a classroom, or an institution all as multilingual. The term *additive multilingualism* is used to describe a situation in which an individual adds a language to their repertoire while continuing to use their first or other languages; in contrast, *subtractive multilingualism* refers to the displacement of one's first language by another language, as often occurs in children in immigrant communities. Multilingualism has many benefits for individuals, including increased metalinguistic awareness and potentially slower cognitive decline with aging (Cenoz, 2013).

It may be easy to imagine that a multilingual person simply adds and compartmentalizes additional languages beyond their first. Instead, the construct of multicompetence describes the multilingual as having a holistically different mind, in which all of the person's languages form an interrelated system and affect cognition as a whole (Cook, 1992, 2012). In other words, the multilingual user has "a compound state of linguistic knowledge that is different from the combined knowledge of two or more monolingual language users" (Rinnert & Kobayashi, 2016, p. 365). One key premise of multicompetence, Cook (2012) argues, is that the norm for L2 acquisition research should be L2/multilingual users *not* monolingual "native speakers" because the two are fundamentally different. By extension, L2 classrooms should define success not in relation to a perceived "native speaker" ideal but instead in relation to competent and successful L2 users (Cook, 2012). From this perspective, a multilingual teacher brings ideal experience to an L2 classroom.

Research into multilingualism and multicompetence in L2 writing is still in its early stages but has begun to illuminate some of the unique aspects of multilingual writing. For example, findings suggest that experienced multilingual writers do not typically transfer their knowledge of writing features in one language to another but instead draw on a combined system of knowledge about writing across languages (Rinnert & Kobayashi, 2016). As such, multilingual writers generally have a broader repertoire of discursive, rhetorical, and linguistic resources available to them than monolingual writers (Canagarajah, 2006; Rinnert & Kobayashi, 2016). Research continues to explore how language proficiency, writing proficiency, and genre knowledge interact for multilingual writers (Gentil, 2011).

A related, even overlapping, perspective is that of translingualism or translanguaging. Translanguaging, like multicompetence, recognizes the holistic nature of a multilingual repertoire and further emphasizes the fluidity of language practices (Cenoz & Gorter, 2021). In writing studies, the term *translingualism* has often been used to describe a disposition toward language as a heterogeneous and fluid resource for meaning making, which is embedded in structures of power (Horner et al., 2011). Though the premises of translingualism are, in my view, consistent with contemporary views of language in L2 writing, scholars still hold disagreements regarding the practicality and appropriateness of translingual pedagogy, especially in the context of L2AW (see, for example, Silva & Wang, 2021). A key question involves what it means, in practice, to question or challenge dominant norms in an L2AW classroom.

There are many important implications of taking a multilingualism-as-a-resource perspective to L2AW, whether it is through the lens of multilingualism or translingualism. Such a perspective identifies a valuable role for all of students' languages in the L2AW classroom, as an aid to some of the cognitive demands of multilingual writing, as a validation of students' languages and varieties, and as a motivator (Gentil, 2018; Rinnert & Kobayashi, 2016). Use of writers' multiple languages, particularly when comparing texts and practices across languages, can also support metacognitive awareness and transfer of writing knowledge across languages and contexts (Gentil, 2018).

3.3 Discourse and Discourse Community

Discourse is another term with multiple definitions. In relation to literacy, discourse is often described, following Gee (1989), as a kind of identity kit, or as "*saying (writing)-doing–being–valuing–believing combinations*" (p. 6). Discourses can be tied to professions (medical discourse, legal discourse), interest groups (crafting discourse, skateboarding discourse), or communities that share a physical space (institutional discourse). Though discourses are broad practices, they can also be identified and analyzed at the level of written text.

Discourses are highly social, which is why Gee's (1989) emphasis on identity as part of discourse is so valuable. The written (and spoken) patterns associated with particular discourses reflect aspects of a social group's identity, including the topics that are of interest and importance, their specialist knowledge on those topics, and the group's values in terms of how ideas are communicated and—in the case of academic discourse—how knowledge is constructed.

The term *discourse community* refers to a community of people who share certain ways of using language to carry out a shared social practice (Bizzell, 1992; Swales, 1990). For example, the community may be people who share a hobby such as rock climbing or painting, or they may share a profession such as nursing or musical performance. Discourse communities can be place based (e.g., people who share an office area or communal living space) or interest based, with members communicating primarily in virtual spaces or at special events like conferences (Swales, 1998). In L2AW instruction, discourse community offers a framework for understanding how writing is shaped by the people who use it. For example, students can explore how different communities (such as academic disciplines) are similar and different in their practices, including what they write and how they write. Such communities may be as small and temporary as a classroom or as vast and slowly changing as an academic discipline.

A large body of research has analyzed features of written academic discourse, generally driven by a desire to understand patterns so that they can be taught to students. For example, research has highlighted patterns of stance (Hyland, 2005), citation use (Hyland, 1999), and metadiscourse (language that organizes texts and engages directly with readers) (Hyland & Tse, 2005). While many of these features can be studied at the discourse level (that is across numerous genres within a discourse), they are often also studied at the level of genre (see section 3.4). Such research has important implications for L2AW, offering insights into patterns of writing and raising students' awareness into the variability of writing.

Because discourse is a social practice, learning a discourse involves learning to participate in and identify with a social group (a discourse community). In the case of academic discourse, this involves being (or hoping to be) part of an academic community, perhaps even a more specific disciplinary community, and gradually developing an identity as someone who is a part of the group. When learners feel alienated or distant from a community, they may struggle with or even resist adopting its discourse, and they eventually may even choose not to participate in the group (Casanave, 2005). To support students in learning the social practices of academic discourse, some practitioners have advocated for incorporating interviews with experts or ethnography-like exploration of academic discourse as part of L2AW instruction (e.g., Johns, 1997; Johns et al., 2006).

Reflection

1. Identify at least two different kinds of texts that you have written in the past week or so, with at least one being an example of academic writing (as you understand it). For example, you may have written academic texts like an academic paper, job application letter, grant proposal, or conference abstract; you may have written nonacademic texts such as a social media post, a text thread with a friend, a letter of complaint, or an email thanking someone. Look at the language that you used in these two texts in terms of the grammar and word choices. What aspects of language do you notice being similar or different? In what ways do your two texts illustrate that writing involves controlling a broad repertoire of language?

2. Look again at the same texts and consider how they might relate to the concepts of discourse and discourse community. What functions do they carry out, and how do language choices help them do so? What communities use these texts? To what extent does using these texts mark you as a particular "kind of person" or a member of a particular discourse community?

3. Consider a discourse community that you are a part of. What are some examples of how that community uses language in unique ways (such as specific jargon or unique ways of speaking/writing)? How does someone learn these ways of using language? How did you learn this?

Teaching Second Language Academic Writing 21

3.4 Genre

Discourse and genre are closely related. To adopt an analogy, genres might be likened to the animal life in a body of water, with discourse being the water they live in. While discourse surrounds us, genre takes more specific shapes—as Bakhtin (1986) notes, a genre has a beginning, a middle, and an end.

In writing and language studies, genre refers to a category of texts that share a social action (a functional or rhetorical goal) (Miller, 1984; Swales, 1990). Examples of everyday genres include apology emails, complaint letters, grocery lists, and retirement speeches. In specialized settings, discourse communities develop preferred forms for accomplishing their activities and goals; in other words, they develop their own genres. Knitters use conventionalized patterns to share instructions with a wide audience, nurses use nursing care plans to communicate a patient's needs to them and to other nurses, and politicians use political ads to persuade people to vote for them. Each of these kinds of writing may be difficult or impossible for outsiders to understand, but for community members they become a valuable communication tool. Importantly, genres are different from the templates or predetermined forms or structures that are frequently taught in school. While writing formulas can provide scaffolding to writers, they are rigid and static. In contrast, genres evolve over time (compare, for example, a love letter from the 1800s to one today!), and they adapt to each unique use, so that they display variation both diachronically and synchronically (Tardy et al., 2023).

Students gradually expand the repertoire of genres in which they read and write as they progress through their education. In advanced secondary school and in higher education, students encounter genres like personal statements, lab reports, science posters, literary analyses, and grant proposals. At the tertiary level, education gradually becomes increasingly discipline-specific and so too the genres.

Because so much written communication occurs through genres, some have argued that "there is no such thing as writing in general" (Wardle, 2017, p. 30). Instead, the success of a text is highly dependent on the degree to which it fulfills its specific readers' expectations for the genre. In an L2AW class, the concept of genre can help students understand how writing adapts to a situation, including the audience/community, the goal(s), and other aspects of the context. A genre perspective allows students to see that text forms are not static and random but instead are a result of a community's practices, expectations, and histories.

Like learning a discourse, learning genres is in part a social process. We often develop control over genres through watching others use them and eventually doing so ourselves. With exposure, practice, and feedback many genres can be learned in this implicit manner. For more complex genres (most academic genres), however, research suggests that learners benefit from explicit instruction that guides them to explore common conventions and variations within a genre (e.g., Cheng, 2008; Yasuda, 2011). Writers can develop their understanding of and ability to use unfamiliar genres through exploration of samples (or "mentor texts"), feedback from instructors or more experienced users, and collaborative writing (Caplan & Farling, 2017; Hyland, 2007).

Sophisticated understanding of a genre requires writers to develop complex knowledge: an understanding of the specific genre (including the subject-matter content of the texts, as well as how texts in the genre are produced and distributed; effective ways to appeal to the given audience, goals, and settings; and successful choices in textual forms) and metacognitive knowledge of how writing and genres work, also referred to as genre awareness (Tardy et al., 2020). These two aspects of genre knowledge (genre-specific knowledge and genre awareness) work together. For example, a student requires knowledge of the lab report genre in order to write a lab report. If the student is then asked to create a scientific poster describing the same lab experiment, their knowledge of the lab report will only help so much. The student's genre awareness is also essential in helping them adapt their genre-specific knowledge to the creation of a scientific poster.

Multilingual academic writers may feel that they are at a disadvantage in learning academic genres in an additional language, compared with classmates using their first language. One potential challenge for multilinguals is that genres can function and look different across languages and cultural settings. Yet, an understanding of this very disconnect—the variations in how genres are used and written—can also bolster multilinguals' genre awareness. In other words, multilinguals personally experience genre shifts as they traverse cultural and linguistic communities, likely enhancing their metalinguistic and genre awareness (Gentil, 2011).

These scholarly conceptions of genre and genre knowledge make a strong case for teaching students more than formulas (see Caplan & Johns, 2019) and for raising writers' awareness of the critical role of audience or discourse community and social functions or actions in writing and evaluating texts.

3.5 Rhetoric

Rhetoric is a term with numerous scholarly definitions. For Aristotle, rhetoric is related to how writers or orators understand and appeal to their audience in a particular setting—that is, how they locate the available means of persuasion in a given situation. In academic writing, a focus on rhetoric generally includes consideration of how writers appeal to, engage with, or even change the minds of their readers. Rhetorical choices can be linguistic (such as the decision of how formal grammar or lexis should be), but they can also relate to content (e.g., the use of personal examples, or the use of praise or criticism when referring to published work), design features (e.g., whether or how many levels of headings to use, or where and how to incorporate visuals), or distribution practices (e.g., publishing in a local versus international journal, publishing in a local or international language). Roozen (2016) provides a helpful definition of rhetoric for writing teachers:

> Considering writing as rhetorical helps learners understand the needs of an audience, what the audience knows and does not know, why audience members might need certain kinds of information, what the audience finds persuasive (or not), and so on. Understanding the rhetorical work of writing is essential if writers are to make informed, productive decisions about which genres to employ, which languages to act with, which texts to reference, and so on. Recognizing the deeply social and rhetorical dimensions of writing can help administrators and other stakeholders make better decisions about curricula and assessment. (p. 19)

Learning which rhetorical choices are common in different kinds of academic writing can be challenging for any student, regardless of language background. But rhetorical preferences also tend to vary across linguistic and cultural contexts, so writers may need to learn new preferences when writing in new contexts. To take one insightful example, academic letters of recommendation written in British English can differ rhetorically from those written in American English, with British letters often including a negative critique that recognizes the recommendee's limitations and thereby offers a more realistic assessment (Precht, 1998); in American letters, inclusion of such a move would likely signal the recommender's extreme hesitation about the applicant!

Research suggests that rhetorical knowledge is often learned through participation in discourse communities and through mentorship (Tardy, 2005). As a kind of metacognitive awareness, rhetorical knowledge can be adapted across educational spaces (Wardle, 2007); however, such adaptation requires, or at least is greatly facilitated by, explicit instruction and guidance in "disciplinary writing values, beliefs, genres, expectations, and practice" (Nowacek et al., 2024, p. 222).

Given these research insights, L2AW classrooms should aim to develop students' rhetorical knowledge throughout instruction. Earlier and general contexts of L2AW instruction may include attention to broad academic audiences, with an increasingly specific audience focus as writers' needs become more specialized by discipline or profession. Johns (2009) has argued that a primary goal of L2AW instruction should be to foster writers' *rhetorical flexibility*, referring to their ability to adapt their writing to an ever-growing and unpredictable set of audiences and purposes.

3.6 Academic Literacies

It may be argued that learning to write in academic contexts is in many ways unique. Not only are students asked to read and write in genres that are rarely used outside of educational settings but the writing that they do carries out specific purposes and is typically read within a hierarchical dynamic in which teachers assess students. Academic literacies is an orientation or movement which aims to understand student learning in this very specific and complex setting.

Early work in academic literacies (or Ac Lits) grew out of conversations related to expanded student populations in higher education in the UK and South Africa. Practitioners began questioning common deficit-driven approaches to literacy, which situated students as lacking skills and which overlooked the role of power and ideology in institutional learning (Lillis & Tuck, 2016). Ac Lits begins with the premise that literacies are not simply skills but are also social practices. These social practices are developed and carried out within institutions, which are themselves contested "sites of discourse and power" (Lea & Street, 1998, p. 158). Within these complex sites, students must learn to "deploy a repertoire of linguistic practices appropriate to each setting, and to handle the social meanings and identities that each evokes" (p. 158). A challenging task indeed, but one that is often crucial for success in academic environments.

Viewing academic literacies as inherently social, epistemological, and ideological, Ac Lits is also explicitly critical. Rather delaying an interrogation of academic practices until more advanced stages of writing, criticality is a key component of Ac Lits at any stage (Lillis & Tuck, 2016). Toward this aim, Ac Lits emphasizes the notion of transformativity, as a contrast to normativity. For instance, an Ac Lits approach encourages transformation of academic writing itself, including which linguistic and semiotic resources are considered appropriate to use and what categories like "English" and "academic" can encompass (Lillis & Tuck, 2016).

Lillis and Tuck (2016) identify several key themes in Ac Lits research:

- Expectations in academic settings are often made mysterious (by institutions) to students;

- Disciplinary approaches to writing and research practices are variable, dynamic, and contested;
- Identity is important to academic writing, including which identities are "sanctioned" and valued in different spaces;
- Certain linguistic and semiotic resources have historically been valued over others in academic contexts, limiting access to and enrichment of knowledge production; and
- Practices for text production in academic and professional contexts are transforming in the digital age.

Together, these themes depict Ac Lits as an orientation to literacy which seeks to challenge normative practices and open academic spaces to diverse voices and practices. This perspective challenges L2AW teachers and students to not simply accept academic writing norms as they are, but also to imagine and produce alternatives that may open up academic spaces to more voices.

3.7 Multimodality

For many people, academic writing is associated with written words—and lots of them. Words most certainly form the foundation of much academic writing, and they often represent some of the most challenging aspects of academic writing. But written text is only one of the modes through which academic writers can express ideas and communicate knowledge. According to Kress (2017), a mode is "a socially shaped and culturally given resource for meaning-making. Image, writing, layout, music, gesture, speech, moving image, and soundtrack are examples of modes used in representation and communication" (p. 60). Texts that combine two or more of these modalities can be considered multimodal. Examples of multimodal academic writing include papers that incorporate any kind of table, chart, graph, or image; presentation slides that blend text, video, color, and image; or a video abstract that relies on a written script, speech, moving image, and perhaps even music.

Multimodality, as we understand it today, is often traced to Halliday's (1978) *Language as a Social Semiotic*, where Halliday emphasized that humans make meaning through a range of semiotic resources, of which language is one. Subsequently, scholars like Kress and van Leeuwen (1996) and Jewitt (2006) further developed more in-depth theories of such resources under the umbrella of multimodality. Despite its roots in Hallidayan linguistics, scholars in the field of composition studies embraced multimodality earlier than those in L2 writing (though rarely through an explicitly Hallidayan lens). Even in the 2010s, scholars debated in print the extent to which multimodal composing has a role in the L2 writing classroom (e.g., Belcher, 2017; Manchón, 2017). It is understandable to feel that multimodality should take up less space in one's L2AW classrooms compared to the written word (Qu, 2017), but it is also difficult to argue against Yi et al.'s (2020) assertion that "Reading and writing multimodal texts are a *necessity* in contemporary communication" (p. 1).

Apart from its ubiquity, there are many reasons to bring multimodality into the L2AW classroom. Importantly, with its opportunities for creativity and individuality, multimodal composing can be engaging and motivating to students (Belcher, 2023; Sun et al., 2021). Research into multimodal composing has also shown that it offers L2 writers more and varied opportunities to express their identities, that the collaboration often involved in multimodal composing can help expand students' linguistic repertoires, and that the nonlinguistic modes students use can serve as additional learning resources (Smith et al., 2021). There may also be more direct contributions to writing development, as a study by Kim et al. (2023) found that students composing digital multimodal texts produced longer texts and showed greater gains in writing development compared with students who produced traditional writing. Given the importance and potential benefits of multimodal writing, L2AW teachers can consider where and how it may fit in their instruction, whether in low-stakes activities or in major writing tasks.

3.8 Culture

Culture is perhaps one of the least defined and most contested concepts relevant to L2AW. Drawing on Ruth Benedict (1936), Atkinson (2016) defines culture as a "'more or less consistent pattern of thought or interaction' to which 'the life history of the individual is first and foremost an accommodation" (p. 546).

The role of culture in L2AW was first highlighted in the 1960s by Kaplan (1966), who explored how cultural preferences may shape rhetorical aspects of writing. Kaplan referred to these variations as "cultural thought patterns" and illustrated some of the ways these patterns can differ across languages. For example, Kaplan depicted writing in some languages as following a circular pattern of thought, while writing in English was represented with a straight line. In comparing how languages may organize ideas, Kaplan drew attention to this less visible aspect of multilingual writing, which he referred to as contrastive rhetoric. Though now often viewed as overgeneralized, contrastive rhetoric was pioneering at the time because it brought attention to influences on L2 writers' texts beyond grammar or lexicon.

Contrastive rhetoric and attention to culture in L2AW has developed considerably since the 1960s. Culture, for example, is no longer equated with a homogenous national culture; instead, scholarship recognizes "big cultures" (e.g., national culture, youth culture) and "small cultures" (e.g., classroom cultures, disciplinary culture) which intersect and overlap (see Atkinson, 2004, drawing on Holliday, 1994). Contrastive rhetoric is now more commonly referred to as intercultural rhetoric and emphasizes the contexts, processes, and multiplicities of culture involved in text production much more than static textual products (Connor et al., 2016). In addition, numerous scholars have offered alternative visions of culture for second language studies, specifically turning to more critical and pluralistic views that highlight how culture is bound relationally to rhetoric, power, and discourse (e.g., Kubota, 2002; Kubota & Lehner, 2004). A multilingual writer, for example, may choose to foreground or background various cultural and rhetorical strategies when writing in and across different communities (e.g., Canagarajah, 2006). From this perspective, L2AWs' cultural resources play a valuable role in textual ownership and identity.

L2AW teachers can also help student writers to view culture in this dynamic and plural manner. Students can be encouraged to explore how they can adapt their writing when communicating across big and small cultural communities as well as how their layered and rich cultural knowledge adds to their writing knowledge.

3.9 Identity

Unfortunately, for many years, second language writing research tended to ascribe fairly rigid and restrictive identities to L2 writers, limited primarily to countries of origin and first languages. An emergence of more qualitative research in the 1990s and onward helped to bring more complex awareness of writers' identities (e.g., Blanton, 1994; Severino, 1993), and new theoretical work on identity (e.g., Peirce, 1995) also contributed to a more nuanced view of who learners are. Following a poststructuralist orientation, Norton (Peirce, 1995) re-situated identity from being stable and singular to plural, dynamic, and social. Linking identities to social groups helps to highlight how our participation in a community (including the community's writing practices) allows us to perform and construct identities associated with that community (Hyland, 2012); on the other hand, if our performed identities do not align with the community, we may be seen as an outsider.

Identity is deeply intertwined with academic writing. Ivanič (1998) made significant strides in elaborating this relationship through a theory of identity and writing that recognized that writers have multiple identities, such as their more personal autobiographical identities and the identities that are constructed through the genres and discourses that they use as writers. Drawing heavily on Bakhtin (1986), Ivanič also emphasized that writers develop their identities or voices as they read and interact with others and then remix or reenact those voices for their own purposes.

Voice has been an important area of interest in its own right in L2AW, though it is closely tied in theory and practice to writing identity. In Matsuda's (2001) definition, voice is "the amalgamative effect of the use of discursive and non-discursive features that language users choose, deliberately or otherwise, from socially available yet ever-changing repertoire" (p. 40). Research into voice has emphasized two parts of this definition: writers' *choices* in using discursive and nondiscursive features and the *effect* of those choices. For instance, readers (teachers, community members) construct the voice of a writer through features of writing (e.g., vocabulary, grammar, organization, formatting, content) and also through the genre (*Who writes this kind of text?*) and situation (*How should a writer carry out their aim in this context?*). Writers may experience challenges in expressing a desired voice, but instruction can help draw attention to how different writing choices may construct different identities. Research has also highlighted that identities are not constructed only through writers' texts but also through their racial or linguistic identities (Rubin & Williams-James, 1997; Tardy, 2012) and through the sociopolitical contexts (Starfield, 2002). Thus, writer identity is a complicated aspect of writing, over which writers do not have full control.

While much focus on identity in L2AW has been on texts, research has also explored how identity can be deeply implicated in the development of or resistance to academic literacies (e.g., Casanave, 2005; Kibler, 2017; Liu & Tannacito, 2013). In a space in which learners' identities are so intertwined with their learning, L2AW teachers will do well to adopt an intersectional stance toward students' identities and to find ways to recognize and embrace the many identities that students bring to their writing and learning.

3.10 Global Englishes

Following Galloway and Rose (2015), I use *Global Englishes* (GE) as an umbrella term, a kind of paradigm or orientation that encompasses World Englishes, English as a lingua franca (ELF), English as an international language (EIL), plurilingualism, and translanguaging, among other orientations to language which highlight linguistic diversity, local and plural norms, and dispersed ownership of language. Though it is tied to the unique situation of English in a global context, the basic paradigm of GE can also be extended to language learning and use more broadly. Some dimensions of a GE approach in the classroom, outlined by Selvi et al. (2023), include:

- an expansion of target interlocutors and cultures to more fully represent the diversity of English use;
- a pluralization of linguistic norms that are taught and assessed;

- a recognition and strategic use of multiple languages and cultures; and
- an adoption of a critical stance toward English and language.

These dimensions also align with many principles of multilingualism and translingualism (see Section 3.2).

GE has focused primarily on spoken language, which tends to display wide variation in, for example, accents, prosody, vocabulary and slang, conversational pragmatics, and colloquial grammar. In contrast, written language tends to have less tolerance for variability, in part because there is typically no immediate opportunity to repair communication lapses. (The rise of written interactions through texting or social media complicates this dichotomy often considerably.) Academic writing in particular tends to value a tighter adherence to normative language and offer fewer opportunities for local variation. Norms for academic writing are established and reinforced by those with social power (within academic contexts) through gatekeeping in, for example, assessment, admissions, funding decisions, and editorial selection. There is absolutely room for critique here: academic writing norms are rarely established from the ground-up, and indeed they can and do operate to exclude people who are linguistically, racially, socially, and/or economically marginalized. These exclusions happen at least partially through the reinforcement of certain linguistic and rhetorical norms.

L2AW students and teachers may wonder then: Can a paradigm like Global Englishes, with its emphasis on heterogeneity, be compatible with academic writing, which tends to emphasize prestige norms? Valuing linguistic diversity while also recognizing that academic contexts often reward conformity can raise questions for L2AW teachers: Should norms of academic writing be taught and enforced through assessment? If so, which or whose norms? If not, which students will be disadvantaged? In response to these kinds of questions, Matsuda and Matsuda (2010) recommend that L2AW classrooms teach *both* the dominant norms *and* the nondominant variations:

> The diversity of Englishes owes much to the ongoing contact among diverse users of Englishes with users of other Englishes and languages. Every time L2 writers write in English, they are engaging in a language-contact situation. To prepare students adequately in the era of globalization, we as teachers need to fully embrace the complexity of English and facilitate the development of global literacy. (p. 373)

In this view, academic writing instruction must include discussions of linguistic diversity and inequity as well as exploration of strategies for effectively integrating nondominant linguistic and rhetorical choices into academic writing (see, for example, Canagarajah, 2013; Schreiber, 2020).

30 Language Teaching

> ## Reflection
>
> 1. Make a list of the kinds of writing that are commonly taught in L2AW classrooms within contexts you are familiar with. Then, discuss with a partner or group the extent to which these writing types offer students opportunities to compose across genres, including for various audiences and purposes.
> 2. How do concepts like culture, identity, and Global Englishes complicate your understanding of academic writing? To what extent do you feel that academic writing is or should be open to diversification? If you feel that it should be open, how do you think instructors should approach the teaching and assessment of academic writing in the classroom?

4 Approaches in Teaching L2 Academic Writing

Section 3 reviewed some critical concepts in the teaching L2AW. We now turn to look at pedagogical approaches, which offer a coherent means for bringing such concepts into the classroom. Put another way, pedagogical approaches provide teachers a framework for considering how principles of teaching and learning, goals, and strategies can be implemented.

Pedagogical approaches to teaching L2AW are often broadly classified by their relative focus on writers, readers, social contexts, composing, or texts. (See, for example, Hyland, 2019, and Ferris & Hedgcock, 2023.) These taxonomies are not intended to suggest that teachers should choose just one approach. Rather, such categorizations can help teachers reflect on how different approaches align with their teaching values, educational setting, and student goals (as described in Section 1), which of course change over time and perhaps even within a course. In the end, L2AW instruction should address *all* layers of writing (writers, readers, social contexts, composing, and texts), though how teachers do so will vary in relation to their individual setting and philosophies.

This section does not provide an historical or comprehensive overview of L2AW approaches but instead aims to highlight some of the more influential approaches found in L2AW contexts. The focus is on the approaches' goals and principles of learning; an understanding of these goals and principles can contribute to teachers' evolving small-t theories of teaching L2AW. It is important to keep in mind that though the approaches are described one by one in this section, they should be considered complementary tools in a teacher's toolkit. That is, in practice, they are more often than not integrated.

4.1 Process Pedagogy

There is a meme that shows a writer's digital folder with document files labeled something like this:

- Finaldraft.doc
- Newfinaldraft.doc
- Newfinalfinaldraft.doc
- Newfinalistfinaldraft.doc
- Newfinalistfinaldraftforsure.doc
- Newfinalistfinaldraftforsurewhateverimdone.doc

This meme is relatable to most experienced writers, and it is also a wonderful representation of the writing process, which is the foundation of process pedagogy.

Process pedagogy emphasizes the practice of composing and its various stages, in contrast to more traditional approaches to teaching writing which teach toward and grade only a student's end-product. Process pedagogy has its roots in the cognitive study of writing. Pioneering research by Flower and Hayes (1981) used a think-aloud protocol methodology to examine what expert writers do when they write. By asking writers to "think aloud," voicing their thoughts throughout their entire process of composing, researchers can identify multiple stages, including often extensive revision. Based on this kind of research, Flower and Hayes (1981) outlined a cognitive process theory of writing that emphasized the interaction of writer goals and the thinking processes that organize composing. This theory and research had a tremendous impact on writing instruction. If successful writers plan their texts and work through often multiple rounds of revision, then it seems likely that novice writers would also benefit by learning to do the same.

Roughly around the same time as early cognitivist work on writing processes, a separate area of composition studies scholarship emphasized the value of drafting and revision, in what is known as the expressivist movement. Peter Elbow was one of the most influential expressivists; he argued that student writers need to write about topics they care about, and they need to be given time to develop their ideas and sense of ownership over their writing (Elbow, 1973, 1981). In other words, writing was considered primarily a form of self-expression, and writing instructors were encouraged to place higher value on students' ideas and ownership of their writing.

Both the cognitivist and expressivist approaches emphasized the importance of writing processes, though from different theoretical bases. Nevertheless, their work coincided in timing and a shared view of the "importance of learning to write by writing" (Hirvela et al., 2016, p. 47). These early process-oriented views of writing contributed to a fairly substantial shift in writing pedagogy that continues to this day. The goals of process pedagogy are to teach strategies and approaches to writing, including planning, revision, and editing.

Research into process writing in second language writing has been substantial; a comprehensive summary of that work is beyond the scope of this Element. Still, we can glean important principles of learning and teaching from that research, particularly in relation to how multilingual writers' composing process may be unique in relation to their monolingual counterparts. For instance, writers' first or dominant language(s) can play a strategic role in composing in an additional language (Manchón et al., 2007; Murphy & Roca de Larios, 2010), and writers may attend more to linguistic-level choices when writing in an additional language (Schoonen et al., 2009). Such practices and uses of writers' multiple languages, of course, also change with proficiency and even familiarity with different kinds of writing (Roca de Larios et al., 2016). At the same time, research generally suggests that writers' strategic composing processes can transfer across their languages, though they may be constrained by linguistic limitations (Cumming, 2016). More recent research on writing processes is also raising awareness of how composing is impacted by technology, including the use of digital and multimodal technology (e.g., Kessler, 2020; Tan, 2023) and artificial intelligence (Zhao, 2023).

A process-oriented L2AW classroom gives writers time and space to plan, draft, revise, edit, and reflect on their work—and to do so while engaging all their linguistic resources. Activities that support these (nonlinear) stages of composing might include freewriting, outlining, mind-mapping, peer review, self-assessment, revising based on feedback, and self-editing, any of which may make purposeful use of a writer's multiple languages. These practices of multilingual composing can be—and often are—explicitly taught, so that students learn how to incorporate composing strategies and reflect on how different strategies enhance their development as writers.

In the classroom, process approaches may also assess process components (such as revision and peer review), further emphasizing for students the importance of these practices. Portfolios offer another form of assessment that can help emphasize the importance of writing process over product; in this case, students revise and compile their best work into a portfolio that typically makes up a major component of their course grade (see, for example, Crusan & Ruecker, 2022). Process can also be emphasized through the assessment approach of ungrading, in which students' grades are de-emphasized, while students' reflection on their learning and extensive instructor feedback become the primary focus (see, for example, Crusan, 2024; Stommel, 2020).

Teaching Second Language Academic Writing 33

4.2 Genre-Based Teaching

Today, few writing scholars and practitioners would deny that process is a critical part of writing or that it deserves a prominent place in writing instruction. Yet, the process of writing is rarely the sole focus of an L2AW classroom, as it may have been at one time. Much writing instruction now also aims to develop students' understanding of the tight relationship between texts and their contexts of use. Writing a clever social media profile, for example, is quite distinct from writing a grant proposal or a science poster or an opinion piece in a school newspaper. Different kinds of writing are typically referred to as *genres* (see Section 3).

When it comes to a focus on texts, academic writing classrooms (and especially L2AW classrooms) have traditionally focused on template-like structures, such as description, argument, analysis, problem-solution or compare-and-contrast. In the 1980s and 1990s, several scholars in applied linguistics (Martin, 1992; Swales, 1990) and rhetoric and composition (Bazerman, 1988; Miller, 1984) began exploring an alternative to this more formulaic approach to structure: genre. Genre is typically theorized as a social or rhetorical *practice*—a community's typical or preferred way of doing something to carry out a goal or action. In academic contexts, written genres include texts as diverse as case studies, narrative essays, review papers, response papers, discussion posts, lab reports, proposals, annotated bibliographies, research articles, and even theses and dissertations (e.g., Nesi & Gardner, 2012).

Genre-based pedagogy is an approach to writing instruction that teaches students how to write in ways that are responsive to the setting, audience/ community of users, and goals. This can involve learning features of specific genres, but it also includes learning how writing choices are tied to contexts. When students are taught tools and processes to analyze genres and their contexts (and the relationship between the two), they are better equipped to adapt their writing for ever-changing situations (e.g., Cheng, 2018; Hyon, 2017; Swales, 1990; Tardy, 2019). Genre-based teaching can also emphasize the learning of the social literacy practices that are part of academic writing (Johns, 1997). A genre-based classroom is thus characterized by students taking on the role of discourse analysts, learning about the communities, practices, and genres of interest and developing skills to adapt such knowledge in unique tasks.

Genre-based pedagogy has parallel origins in three distinct contexts: K–12 education in Australia, English for academic purposes (EAP), and US under-graduate composition. The primary differences in these practices relate to their relative attention to language, though they also have somewhat distinct theoret-ical frameworks. What they share is an understanding that writing is about communication and that communities (often referred to as discourse communities) tend to develop generally agreed-upon ways of communicating. The implication of this understanding is that writing is fundamentally social and therefore also highly variable—*good* writing depends on goals, the users, the setting, the modality, and so on. Teaching students only a small number of structures for writing therefore falls short in helping them develop the rhetorical and linguistic flexibility needed to write across the many genres and communities they will encounter in academic settings and beyond. The goals of genre-based pedagogy are to raise students' awareness (or rhetorical consciousness) of how writing works in general as well as within the settings and genres that are important for them (Cheng, 2018; Hyon, 2017). Put another way, the primary focus of genre-based teaching is not to teach genres per se (though that is part of a genre-based classroom) but rather to develop students' awareness of how writing responds to situations and to help them build strategies for analyzing the situations and genres they encounter and for adapting this knowledge as needed (see also Tardy, 2019; Tardy et al., 2023).

With its focus on exploring how language and rhetoric are used to carry out writers' goals, genre-based teaching relies on inductive learning through exploration of language, texts, and contexts (Cheng, 2018). For example, a teacher may share three examples of a proposal and ask students to look at which different sections the three texts include and reflect on how these choices might relate to the text's audience and content. Or students may analyze the writers' use of hedges (*may, could, might, perhaps*) in the proposals to see how bold or tentative authors are about their claims, or perhaps where in the proposals they use more or fewer hedges. Discovery-oriented activities like these help students develop a metacognitive knowledge of language, rhetoric, and writing by analyzing written forms and relating form to contextual goals (Devitt, 2004).

In a genre-based L2AW classroom, students look at many examples of texts, but they also learn about the communities who use those texts. Classroom tasks may include language analysis, rhetorical analysis, even interviews with writers. Genre-based classrooms may also include many writing tasks that help to strengthen students' genre knowledge and their ability to adapt that knowledge. For example, students may imitate common conventions in a genre but also practice adapting texts to variations in audience, modality, or purpose. They might rewrite a proposal into a presentation slidedeck and then reflect on how and why they modified the text for the new genre. Engaging students in playful manipulation of texts, such as parodies or genre bending or blending, can also help develop their genre knowledge while emphasizing that writing is not static or formulaic but rather responds to ever-changing environments (Hyon, 2017; Tardy, 2016).

4.3 Corpus-Based Teaching

Many of us have seen textbooks which teach language structures that are rarely used or that may seem inappropriate or rare in certain settings. Corpus-based teaching is in many ways a response to such instruction. Early corpora—defined as "systematically collected, naturally occurring categories of texts" (Friginal, 2018, p. 11)—were limited by the technology constraints of the 1960s and 1970s, with the largest of these including a million words from 500 texts (Egbert et al., 2020). Today's large corpora can include billions of words (Egbert et al., 2020), allowing language researchers to learn a great deal about how language is actually used in different situations. For example, corpus analysis can tell us which lexical items or grammar structures (or lexicogrammatical features) are common (or rare) in registers like news articles, conversational speech, or academic writing. Often, such analyses reveal surprising patterns of use or frequency that contradict textbook materials. Corpus-based teaching draws on such insights to engage learners with the various ways that language is actually used and adapted.

Broadly, corpus-based teaching is grounded in an understanding of language as systematic and of corpus research as providing "relevant and meaningful data" (Friginal, 2018, p. 6) for teaching and learning. Flowerdew (2017) highlights *frequency* as a fundamental principle of corpus research and its applications to teaching—that is, the frequency of a linguistic feature or pattern indicates that it may be more important for learners. Like genre-based pedagogy, corpus-based pedagogy also draws on a functional view of language, in which language choices are understood to be tied to the goals and social setting of language use. This principle makes corpus approaches especially well suited to the teaching and learning of academic writing, where text preferences are closely tied to audience, purpose, and context.

Corpus-based teaching is a kind of data-driven learning (DDL) (Johns, 1991), in which students use language data to discover patterns of use that can inform their own linguistic choices. Flowerdew (2023) describes two primary uses of corpora in writing instruction: (1) a *corpus-informed approach*, in which corpus data is used to create instructional materials, and (2) a *corpus-driven approach*, in which students directly interact with a corpus for analysis. As a kind of DDL, corpus-based teaching draws on principles of noticing and inductive learning, as students study data, discuss observations, and inductively derive rules from that data (Charles, 2018; Flowerdew, 2017); such an approach also promotes more independent learning (Flowerdew, 2023) and can lead to better retention of learning (Reppen, 2010).

Corpora used in language teaching can be of varying sizes, depending on the goals of the instruction. For example, a very large and general *reference corpus* offers a broad representation of a language, including multiple registers; the British National Corpus (BNC) is one example. In the L2AW classroom, teachers are more likely to use a *specialized corpus*, which is compiled to represent a more specific context, such as academic abstracts or grant proposals (Friginal, 2018). The English as a Lingua Franca in Academic Settings (ELFA) and the Corpus of Written English as a Lingua Franca in Academic Settings (WrELFA) (English as a Lingua Franca in Academic Settings, n.d.) are examples of specialized corpora that include texts from international academic contexts where English users are from diverse language backgrounds and English is used as the common language of communication (see Mauranen, 2012; Wu & Lei, 2022).

Specialized corpora can also include *learner corpora*, "texts produced by students, regardless of language background, not only in language learning contexts but other learning contexts as well (such as writing instruction)" (Staples et al., 2023). Two examples of learner corpora relevant to L2AW in English are the Michigan Corpus of Upper-Level Student Papers (MICUSP) (2009) and the Corpus and Repository of Writing (CROW) (Staples & Dilger, 2018). A learner corpus can be used to compare student and "expert" texts, or, taking a more asset-based orientation, can be used to illustrate for students common patterns of use among learners similar to them who are writing in similar genres or tasks (Staples et al., 2023). For example, when writing a literature review L2AW students may explore patterns of citation use, hedging, or reporting verbs in a corpus of literature reviews produced by similar students.

Corpus-based materials and activities guide students through exploration of patterns of use and the application of their learning to their own writing. Poole (2016) and Staples et al. (2023) offer two examples of using corpus-informed materials (form specialized corpora) in college-level L2AW instruction.

4.4 Multiliteracies

Responding to the rapid pace of change in late-20th century literacy practices, including "the multiplicity of communications channels and media, and the increasing saliency of cultural and linguistic diversity" (New London Group, 1996, p. 63), a group of scholars known as the New London Group theorized the notion of *multiliteracies*. In their now well-known article, they described a multiliteracies pedagogy, which views language and other meaning-making modalities as dynamic resources that can be exploited by users "to achieve their

Teaching Second Language Academic Writing   37

various cultural purposes" (New London Group, 1996, p. 64). They identified linguistic, visual, audio, gestural, spatial, and multimodal forms of meaning as *design elements*, recognizing the increasing interaction of these elements in textual production. Of course, this intertextuality and multimodality is even more significant today.

Multiliteracies, as both a theoretical framework and pedagogical approach, has developed since its origins in the 1990s. What were originally described as four components of a multiliteracies approach (situated practice, overt instruction, critical framing, and transformed practice) are now described in terms of knowledge processes (experiencing, conceptualizing, analyzing, and applying) which should be integrated in instruction (Cope & Kalantzis, 2015; Kalantzis & Cope, 2010):

- **Situated practice/experiencing**: Because of the situated and contextualized nature of cognition, teaching should weave together in- and out-of-school learner experiences.
- **Overt instruction/conceptualizing**: Students learn to build a conscious awareness of literacy or design elements; metalanguage plays an important role in this process.
- **Critical framing/analyzing**: Learners critique what they learn about texts and their functions in relation to larger social structures and ideologies.
- **Transformed practice/applying**: Students begin to transform practices in diverse real-world contexts to support their own values and needs.

Multiliteracies encompasses multimodality, linguistic and cultural diversity, globalization, and technologies; however, in (L1-oriented) writing studies, the scope is often narrowed to digital literacies and multimodality (Khadka, 2019). Multiliteracies has also gathered attention specifically in non-English foreign language instructional contexts (e.g., Allen, 2018; Kern, 2000), which tend to emphasize meaning making through the use of multiple modalities (especially the intertwined nature of reading, writing, and speaking) and critical perspectives on and language in social contexts (Paesani et al., 2015).

In an L2AW classroom, a multiliteracies approach may include practices such as creative or personal writing ("experiencing"), analyzing genres ("conceptualizing"), reflective writing ("analyzing"), or genre reformulation ("applying") (Paesani et al., 2015; see also Kalantzis & Cope, 2024). Critique and production of digital multimodal texts (a practice that is expanded on in the next section) is also part of a multiliteracies approach (Jiang & Hafner, 2024; Lee et al., 2019). The approach is also, notably, an explicitly inclusive pedagogy, which adopts a critical stance toward power and justice and an emphasis on the importance of access through education. Cope and Kalantzis (2023) emphasize that multiliteracies "represents a broader social agenda of emancipation grounded in the ethics of inclusive sociability and, notwithstanding our differences, our common humanity" (p. 30).

4.5 Social Justice Pedagogies

Since the 1980s, many areas of writing studies scholarship have become increasingly critical in their orientation, arguably influenced in part by the New London Group's pioneering work on multiliteracies. In the US context, another landmark publication in this trajectory was the *Students' Right to Their Own Languages* resolution, also known as *SRTOL*, published by the Conference on College Composition and Communication (CCCC) in 1974. *SRTOL* argued that the aim of writing instruction should not be to privilege and reify one variety of written communication while subordinating or excluding others; instead, linguistic diversity should be validated, and students should be supported in *adding to* their existing linguistic repertoires (Conference on College Composition and Communication, 1974).

In the decades since SRTOL, a stream of scholarship and pedagogical approaches in writing studies more broadly have sought to highlight the need to critique and displace dominant ideologies, discourses, and practices that maintain a linguistic hierarchy, perpetuate a deficit view of certain student populations, and adopt a monolingual and homogeneous perspective on language and writing. These approaches are often broadly described as critical or social justice pedagogies.

Second language writing as a field has generally not embraced critical perspectives as much as (L1-oriented) composition studies has (Silva & Leki, 2004), though there is increasing movement in this direction. Instead, research and practice in L2AW, often aligned with EAP, has tended to take a more pragmatic stance toward writing, famously criticized by Pennycook (1997) as one of "vulgar pragmatism" (p. 256). Early versions of critical pedagogy in L2AW can be found in critical EAP (Benesch, 2001) and critical contrastive rhetoric (Kubota & Lehner, 2004), which questioned the reproduction of dominant norms in academic writing.

There is no single critical or social justice pedagogical approach in L2AW today. Rather, numerous approaches emphasize an interrogation of power and a belief that structures of power need not simply be reproduced through instruction. They tend to draw on related but also distinct theoretical frameworks while sharing an aim of challenging and transforming the dominance of a single, normative variety of written language—one that is very often associated

Teaching Second Language Academic Writing

with white, monolingual English users. Frequently, such approaches also highlight the racialized nature of language hierarchies in the academy, viewing academic language as "not a list of empirical linguistic practice but rather a *raciolinguistic ideology* that frames the home language practices of racialized communities as inherently deficient" (Flores, 2020, p. 24).

Common themes in critically oriented L2AW instruction include recognition that language is diverse and evolving, that dominant norms maintain hierarchies of power, that agency and ownership are important aspects of writing development, and that multilingualism is a resource and asset in writing. Multiliteracies, as already mentioned, is one example of a critical approach, with its emphasis on diversity and access. Academic literacies (Section 3.6) similarly offers a framework for not only seeing academic literacy practices as social but also for seeking to change practices to better serve learners. Another instructional approach that has recently attracted interest is Critical Language Awareness (CLA). CLA "invites teachers and researchers to recognize, draw on, and expand students' linguistic knowledge, assets, and capacities (Shapiro & Lorimer Leonard, 2023, p. 3), often through explicit exploration of language, including in students' own writing.

With its attention to students' own linguistic resources, CLA shares some sensibilities with translingualism (Canagarajah, 2013). A translingual approach

> should bring to the classroom as an object of study the processes by which language standards are constructed and enforced, and how they change over time, exposing them as, if not arbitrary, certainly fluid, dynamic, and context-specific. Ultimately, it should offer the students a way of thinking about language standards as something that can be questioned and challenged and then should offer those students who decide they want to challenge or critique linguistic norms the opportunity and the strategies to do so. (Schreiber, 2020, p. 228)

Teachers have shared illustrations of how these principles can be put into practice, sometimes under the label of translingual pedagogies but sometimes using other terminologies such as plurilingual pedagogies (Losey & Shuck, 2022), social justice pedagogy (Schreiber et al., 2021), or decolonizing pedagogy (Canagarajah, 2024). Slinkard and Gevers (2020) describe activities in which they ask undergraduate international students to actively study and critique how language is assessed in their different courses they are taking. They also describe activities that give students opportunities to critically reflect on their own language varieties and to engage in academic (written) dialogues on the teaching of dominant and nondominant varieties of written language. Canagarajah (2024) emphasizes the two-way nature of literacy by situating multilingual students and teachers as collaborators who learn literacy practices from one another and explicitly learn to mesh and negotiate their diverse knowledges and ways of using language.

Given the highly political nature of language and writing in our societies and indeed in academic settings, the increased attention over the years to social justice education in L2AW is a benefit to teachers. Though not all teachers may find themselves in settings where it is possible or desirable to fully embrace a more critical stance to L2AW instruction, most will find valuable and adaptable principles and practices from this orientation.

4.6 Building Our Own Small-T Theories in L2AW

Most likely, some of the approaches described in this section resonate with individual readers more than others. You may see ways in which, for example, a multiliteracies approach aligns especially well with your personal teaching values and can be easily implemented in your classroom context, but perhaps your interest is also piqued by corpus-based teaching and how it can help engage your students in exploration of authentic language use.

The approaches described here can be complementary to one another when integrated into course design and classroom practice. Indeed, most teachers bring together two or more of these approaches. To offer an example, in an online English L2AW course that I codesigned and occasionally teach, we draw on principles and strategies from several of the approaches described in this section. The course, like many undergraduate writing courses, emphasizes aspects of the writing process through attention to strategies for planning, organizing, revising, and self-editing. It also adopts elements of genre-based and corpus-based teaching, engaging students in discovery-based learning in which they draw on sample texts (often from learner corpora) and explore how writers use various linguistic and rhetorical features to carry out their goals in different genres. A multiliteracies approach also informs our course, which asks students to "write" in a variety of modalities and through a range of semiotic resources. For instance, low-stakes activities ask students to create visuals or short videos to represent their understanding of concepts, while one of the major assignments requires students to integrate color, images, and design choices as they remix and repurpose an academic text for a nonacademic audience. Finally, principles of plurilingual pedagogy inform a major assignment in which students compose a text in two languages and then reflect on the linguistic and rhetorical choices they made when writing across languages and communities.

Teaching Second Language Academic Writing 41

Hopefully, this example illustrates the relative ease and value of drawing on principles and practices from multiple approaches to inform L2AW instruction. Learning about, trying out, and reflecting on various teaching approaches contributes to the development of our small-t theories, as discussed in Section 1.2. As teachers, we can identify our values, learn through professional growth and reflective practice, and constantly refine our understanding of why we do what we do—and whether or how we might do otherwise.

Reflection

1. Identify a principle or goal from at least three pedagogical approaches described in this section that you find especially interesting or important for teaching L2AW. Write out those principles or goals. If possible, compare these with colleagues or peers and discuss why you identified these principles or goals as especially important.
2. Considering the list of important pedagogical principles or goals that you wrote out in item #1, make a list of four to five activities that you have tried or would like to try in your own L2AW instruction. How do these activities carry out some of the principles or goals you identified in item #1? In what educational settings do you think these activities would be especially effective? Again, discuss your responses with colleagues or peers if possible.
3. To what extent do critical or social justice orientations have a place in L2AW instruction in general, in your view? What about in your own teaching settings? Discuss your views with a few others and consider what you can learn from different perspectives on this question.

5 Teaching Practices in L2AW

The pedagogical approaches described in Section 4 offer frameworks that integrate theory and practice and offer guiding principles that aid teachers in making instructional choices. Additionally, teachers of L2AW must make choices about common practices in their classroom. For example, what kinds of writing assignments will they include? How and what kind of feedback will be given to students? There are innumerable practices involved in teaching L2AW, but this section focuses on some of the most important broad areas to consider: assignment design, feedback, assessment, collaborative writing, technology, and creativity and play.

5.1 Assignment Design

One of the most significant decisions that teachers make in an academic writing class is deciding *what* students will write, including the kinds of major assignments. Assignment design affects nearly everything in a writing course. Teachers should pay careful attention to how writing assignments are aligned with course outcomes, assessments, and learning activities.

Several considerations impact the design of major writing assignments. Most obviously, assignments should take into account the goals of the course and the needs of the students. A writing course for doctoral students, for example, would most likely focus on different genres than a course for first-year undergraduates. Assignment design should of course consider what students can already do in writing and how they can build on those skills while working toward their goals.

Choice of genre, audience, and purpose is a critical starting point, but other considerations also come into play. Teachers and course designers will want to ask questions like:

- How long is the course and how much time will students have to work on each writing assignment?
- What other writing courses might the students have already taken (and learned) and what will they take in the future?
- What resources are available within and outside of the course to support different kinds of writing? For instance, do students have access to a library with journal articles?
- To what extent should the assignment offer opportunities for conforming to academic norms and/or for challenging them?
- For assignments that might involve field research, observations, or interviews, what kinds of access do students have to these sites or people?
- What technology might be necessary for different assignments, and what access do students have to it?

Though it may be tempting to fall back on more traditional assignments, such as an "argument essay" or "compare-and-contrast paper," teachers should carefully consider some of the limitations of teaching these more formulaic and decontextualized structures for students. These common forms tend to be less sensitive to audience and focus more on using prescribed patterns, so that students lose out on the opportunity to see writing as flexible, dynamic, and situation-dependent (Caplan & Johns, 2019).

In addition to designing assignments that help to build students' rhetorical awareness and responsiveness, teachers should carefully consider how assignments are scaffolded, both in terms of the sequencing of major assignments

Teaching Second Language Academic Writing 43

throughout a course and the set of activities that help students build the necessary skills and practice needed to complete an assignment (Ferris & Hedgcock, 2023). For example, if students in a pre- or early-university L2AW course are writing a response paper tied to an academic article, they will need to be able to:

- Critically read an academic article
- Summarize an academic article
- Use reporting verbs, paraphrasing, and other features of source attribution
- Write critically about the article
- Develop ideas with explanations and/or illustrations
- Organize ideas within paragraphs and the whole text
- Use language that is effective for the target audience

By breaking down what is involved in a larger writing task, teachers can identify what needs to be taught and assessed, and then develop related assignments, activities, and assessment tools accordingly.

Assignment design should also include space for students to reflect on what they have learned, how they can apply that knowledge to other writing, and where they want to continue to develop as a writer. For example, when submitting an assignment, students can take time in class to write a cover sheet in which they write to the teacher about their progress, areas of success, and areas they would revise if they had more time. Alternatively, students can annotate their final texts (perhaps in a copy of the file), making note of specific skills they demonstrated or revisions they made. This kind of metacognitive reflection can facilitate writing development and the transfer or extension of learning (Negretti & McGrath, 2018).

A teacher's role and options in assignment design will vary contextually. In some contexts, teachers are given standardized assignments and may make limited or no changes to them. Even here, teachers can unpack the skills involved and ensure that classroom activities help prepare students for the skills they need to complete the writing task with success. In other contexts, teachers may have a great deal of autonomy in assignment design. In such cases, a thorough reflection on the classroom ecology (as described in Section 1) will be critical in creating assignments that are appropriate for the course and engaging for the students.

5.2 Feedback

In L2AW instruction, feedback constitutes a primary mode of instruction, offering guidance on students' individualized writing progress and needs. Feedback can come from many sources, such as teachers, peers, the writer themselves, and assistive technology. It can also come at any stage of writing, from planning through final assessment. Because feedback is very often individualized, it has the potential to be more timely, personalized, and relevant than more generalized instruction. In many cases, feedback may be one of the only channels of language instruction that L2AW students receive (Polio, 2019).

Broadly speaking, feedback in the context of L2AW refers to response to students' writing that provides information about how successfully their text meets the goals of a particular task or activity. Teachers provide different kinds of feedback on student writing, including broader commentary on a text, in-text comments, and indicators of linguistic errors (typically termed *written corrective feedback* (WCF)). Teacher feedback may be oral, given in a conference or video or audio recording, or it may be written, most often in a digital text but optionally on paper. Feedback can also come from peers, in which students exchange papers with a classmate or group of classmates and share responses to one another's writing. Self-assessment is another form of feedback, in which students critically examine their own writing and set goals or action plans for revision. Finally, technology has increasingly become a source of feedback for students, whether it be for broader commentary on a text or more micro-level editing, from the spelling and grammar checks built into word processors to the use of apps and programs that offer language or structure-related feedback (e.g., Cotos et al., 2020).

There are many ways to provide feedback on writing, and a substantial body of scholarship has studied what kinds of feedback are most effective. Most of this scholarship has focused on teacher (rather than peer) feedback and on error-related feedback rather than commentary on areas like content, development, or organization. A full review of this research is well beyond the scope of this Element, but Ferris and Hedgcock (2023) outline several general principles of effective teacher feedback. Such feedback tends to:

- balance praise and areas for revision and improvement;
- prioritize areas of concern rather than pointing to everything that might benefit from revision;
- provide clear, usable guidance to students but avoids taking ownership over their writing;
- utilize a variety of modalities (oral, written, video/audio) as appropriate for individual students and classes; and
- come from multiple sources rather than relying only on a single teacher.

In relation to WCF, a vast body of research has studied how teachers should best respond to language errors in student writing (see, for example, Bitchener & Ferris, 2012). Again, there is no "one size fits all" approach, but research has generally pointed to value in WCF for student learning and has suggested that selective or prioritized WCF (i.e., focusing on just a few error types of importance) is more valuable to students than comprehensive feedback in which all errors are addressed (Ferris & Hedgcock, 2023). There is some debate about whether it is more effective for teachers to provide direct corrections of errors or indirect corrections in which an error is pointed out but not corrected. It may be the case that direct correction better supports L2 acquisition, while indirect correction better supports writing development (Ferris & Hedgcock, 2023). Still, there are a wide range of variables that may impact the effectiveness of any approach in a specific environment or for an individual, so teachers are advised to consider their options and reflect on and adjust their practice regularly.

There is, as well, the very thorny issue of what counts as an error to be corrected, which is complicated by recognition of language diversity (Lee, 2023). Teachers should consider and discuss with students how they will address linguistic accuracy and why. For instance, teachers might point out departures from a dominant norm but leave it to students to decide whether to retain such features in their writing. Alternatively, teachers can hold a class discussion on language variations and allow students to request an approach to error feedback based on a list of options from the teacher.

Though teacher feedback is perhaps the most common form of feedback, other forms of feedback can also contribute to writers' development. For instance, peers can respond to classmates' texts through written comments in a draft, through a set of written questions about the draft, and/or in a more open-ended discussion in a peer group. Through peer feedback, students gain other readers' perspectives on their texts, close engagement with assessment criteria, and reflection on their own writing (Yu & Lee, 2016). Self-assessment (evaluating one's own writing and identifying areas for revision and growth as well as strength) can also support writing development (Ferris & Hedgcock, 2023). A short self-assessment activity can be assigned, for example, after a peer review. At this time, students will have read their peers' drafts and can often view their own draft from a broader perspective. They can take a few minutes after a peer review to list what they liked about their peers' drafts, what they think they did well, and a short list of areas to revise is an easy self-assessment activity. Technology—especially assistive-AI tools—can also provide students' feedback on their writing. Though students tend to be skeptical of its value, they often see its accessibility (at times and speeds that teachers cannot match) as an important benefit (Barrot, 2023).

To bring all of these kinds of feedback together in a meaningful way, Ferris (2015) suggests teachers develop a response system, "a thoughtfully designed approach to feedback (from various sources) that serves as a central organizing principle of a writing class" (p. 15). The interlinked components of such a system include mechanisms for getting to know students and their needs, assignment and task design, peer review and collaboration, written and in-person teacher feedback (at various stages of the writing process), and regular reflection and self-assessment.

A response system will not look the same for every instructor but instead should be responsive to student needs and contextual affordances and constraints. In many parts of the world and sometimes online, L2AW classes can be quite large, limiting the extent to which teachers can provide individualized feedback. Similarly, practices like peer feedback or technology-assisted feedback may be unusual or even discouraged in some settings, so their use may require discussion or training to help students effectively utilize these forms of feedback. Additionally, some standardized teaching curricula may restrict opportunities for revision, limiting feedback to final products. Teachers will therefore need to carefully consider what forms, sources, and timing of feedback will be practical and useful in their own context. Some more specific questions to consider include:

- At what stage(s) of writing should students receive feedback?
- What should be the focus of the feedback? How can it align with assessment, the assignment goals, and the pedagogical approach?
- What source(s) of feedback are available and appropriate?
- How much or what kind of training should be implemented to make the feedback and its reception more effective?
- For teachers, how much time is available for providing feedback at different stages of the process and at different points in the semester? How can feedback be streamlined to avoid teacher burnout?
- What are the affordances and constraints of different feedback modalities, including in-person conversations, written feedback, and recorded feedback?
- What technologies are available to and enjoyable for students and teachers?
- How can students be supported in using feedback effectively?
- How can students be supported in developing their own skills in self-evaluation and independence as writers?

An example can illustrate how feedback decisions may be guided by such considerations. A teacher may incorporate peer feedback on students' topic ideas, then perhaps ask students to gather AI-based input on their outlines or organizational plans for their paper. After writing a draft, students may partici-pate in a peer review and also receive screencast feedback from their teacher, focused on a few areas tied to the assignment's assessment rubric. Students may also engage in a guided self-assessment of their draft and then bring together the feedback they have received to create a revision action plan before revising. In the final stages of their process, students may work through a self-editing activity, perhaps with technology assistance. Such a process might also engage students in reflections about linguistic variation and nondominant features. A final draft of the assignment will likely also receive teacher feedback, aligned with the assignment rubric. This kind of approach may be effective in a relatively small classroom but would be more challenging in a large classroom. Several of these steps may depend on available technology. Further, the nature of peer feedback may depend on the content expertise that students bring to the assignment; when peers share disciplinary expertise on the topic, they may be able to provide content feedback in a way that the teachers cannot.

5.3 Assessment

Assessment is an inevitable part of instruction, while also being "quite possibly one of the most time-consuming (and scary) but most significant things teachers can do" (Crusan, 2010, p. 5). Most teachers may think of grading when they think of assessment, but assessment does not necessarily result in a score or grade. Feedback on student drafts, for example, is a kind of assessment.

Writing assessment (like assessment generally) can occur through formative and summative assessment. Formative assessment refers to ongoing and often low-stakes assessment that provides learners and teachers with information about students' progress and areas for improvement. In-class activities, short homework assignments, and regular journals or blogs are all examples of tools that may be used for formative assessment. This kind of assessment is also considered assessment for learning (Ferris & Hedgcock, 2023), because its primary goal is to facilitate students' development. Summative assessment is assessment that summarizes learners' achievement of outcomes at the culmination of an assignment, unit, or course. In writing courses, this might include major writing assignments, portfolios, or even writing exams. Most L2AW courses balance formative and summative assessment.

There are many principles of assessment that are important in building a teacher's overall assessment literacy, including the concepts of reliability, validity, practicality, washback, and ethics (Crusan, 2010; Crusan & Ruecker, 2022; Weigle, 2016). When designing and carrying out classroom-based assessment, L2AW teachers should consider several key elements, including:

- The purpose and desired outcomes of the assessment
- The effects of the assessment on student learning
- The assessment criteria and their alignment with the course goals and content
- The tools for assessment (e.g., short assignments, journals, major writing projects, exams, portfolios)
- The approaches to scoring writing, including rubric types or alternative assessment

Each of these areas is deserving of a much fuller discussion than can be included here; several sources offer excellent overviews for teachers (Crusan, 2010; Ferris & Hedgcock, 2023; Weigle, 2002, 2016).

Assessment decisions are usually not straightforward as they are implicated in larger issues of course design and language ideology. In L2AW classrooms, for instance, teachers need to consider what aspects of language and writing they will assess, in relation to what has actually been taught (Matsuda, 2012) and what the goals and expectations for language use are, including potential acceptance of linguistic and rhetorical diversity. Classroom assessment may also be driven by institutional or program policies or standards, which may or may not align with teachers' own assessment philosophies.

Using rubrics to grade student papers with specific criteria is likely the most common form of summative assessment in L2AW classrooms, but there are other approaches too. Some classrooms use portfolio assessment, in which students compile a range of their writing in a course to illustrate their strengths and growth (Crusan & Ruecker, 2022). This practice emphasizes students' learning and their writing repertoires more than their performance on individual tasks. More recently, L2AW teachers have also considered practices that emphasize feedback and learning and de-emphasize scoring and grades. One example is labor-based contract grading, in which students and teachers enter a "contract" for grading expectations based on areas like time spent and number or type of tasks completed; teacher feedback addresses writing quality but that need not be a determinant of the grade (see Sims, 2023, for further discussion). Similarly, ungrading minimizes or even eliminates grades from the assessment equation, instead focusing on student learning and self-reflection, often through robust feedback (Blum, 2020; Crusan, 2024).

Of increasing note in L2AW assessment, as well, is the evolution of technology and its potential as an aid in assessment. Advocates note that AI-driven automated scoring can be more consistent and efficient than human graders (Mizumoto & Eguchi, 2023; Mizumoto et al., 2024), potentially enhancing teacher assessment and feedback. At the same time, the success of such feedback can depend on contextual features such as a student's language proficiency, motivation, and the goals and purposes of the feedback and revisions (Zhang, 2020). There are also ethical questions about the use of AI technologies that individual teachers should seriously engage with when making decisions on its use.

5.4 Collaborative Writing

Writing is often thought of as a personal, even lonely, endeavor. An internet search for "writer" yields images of individuals at their laptops, typewriters, or notepads, often with looks of frustration or determination. But much of the writing in educational and professional settings is collaborative, defined by Storch (2013) as "the co-authoring of a text by two or more writers" (p. 2). It is often characterized by substantial interaction between the coauthors, a resulting single text, and shared ownership among the text's authors (Storch, 2016). Collaborative writing can occur in person or in synchronous or asynchronous digital environments. In classroom settings, collaborative writing can occur in short activities and in major projects.

Despite persistent images of writing as a solitary activity, there are many reasons to incorporate collaborative writing into L2AW instruction. Theoretical support for collaborative writing is found in second language acquisition (SLA) cognitive theories of learning, as well as Vygostksyan sociocultural learning theory. Briefly, SLA cognitive theories identify interaction and output as facilitating language learning. For instance, when interacting with others to produce language, learners negotiate choices of form; in doing so, they focus on form, and consolidate, apply, and reflect on their language knowledge (Storch, 2013). Sociocultural theory further highlights the value of verbal and social interactions in language learning. From a sociocultural perspective, learning is a social process; for instance, users bring their own expertise to different language production tasks and together can help each other accomplish activities that they could not complete alone. Swain's (2000) notion of languaging also provides insight into the value of collaborative writing. Languaging is the act of using language to complete a complex task, essentially to articulate a thought process; it can occur privately or with others. When writers engage in languaging to coproduce a text, they consolidate their language knowledge and resources, scaffold their activity, and jointly construct new knowledge (Storch, 2013).

Aside from theoretical support for collaborative activity in language learning, research into collaborative writing also demonstrates its value. Most studies find that collaboratively produced student writing is more accurate than individually produced texts (Elabdali, 2021; Fernández Dobao, 2012), and in some studies students who participated in collaborative writing scored higher on subsequent writing tasks (Elabdali, 2021). Storch (2016) describes many additional benefits of collaborative writing in instructional settings, including its attention to the writing process, its potential for developing learners' writing knowledge, its opportunities for learners to take on different writer roles, and its preparation for the collaborative writing that is so frequent in workplace settings.

50   *Language Teaching*

Collaborative writing can be implemented in a variety of context-sensitive ways. As Zhang et al. (2021) note in their review of computer-mediated collaborative writing, such collaboration can be adapted to a wide range of genres, modalities, and technological tools. Short collaborative writing can take place in classrooms themselves and may guide students to attend to different aspects of their writing, such as linguistic features, content, or genre expectations. For instance, when learning academic summary writing, students might work together in pairs or triads to write a one-paragraph summary of a reading from class. The task might provide them with a checklist for issues to consider, such as the use of reporting verbs (*The authors **found that** . . .*), effective use of verb tense, or a focus on main ideas versus details. Groups could also compare their texts and the different choices made, and then reflect on what they learned about summary writing. In more substantial collaborative writing activities, teachers may provide clear expectations and guidance to support collaboration. Students could also discuss what effective and ineffective collaborative writing might involve. Some approaches to genre pedagogy emphasize collaborative writing as a crucial part of a teaching/learning cycle that moves students from analyzing a target genre to jointly composing texts in the genre and, finally, to independent writing in the genre (e.g., Caplan & Farling, 2017).

When planning for collaborative writing activities, L2AW teachers can consider their goals, student expectations, necessary preparation or guidance, and modalities and technology that will be needed. Teachers should also carefully consider how collaborative writing—especially for major writing assignments—will be assessed.

5.5 Source Use

One defining characteristic of academic writing is its high level of engagement with other texts. Academic genres incorporate other sources for a variety of purposes, such as:

- To summarize information from other sources
- To synthesize information from other sources
- To establish and add to a scholarly conversation in a particular area of study
- To respond to or critique another source or set of sources

Source use includes several (inter-)related literacy practices (Wette, 2021). For instance, in order to use sources, students need to locate them, which involves learning to use library databases, to scan databases for relevant sources, to skim sources to identify their appropriateness, and to critically evaluate a source's quality and credibility. Students also need to learn rhetorical

Teaching Second Language Academic Writing 51

strategies for integrating sources into their writing, such as when and how to attribute sources. There are different citation types, including integral citations like *Xu (2024) found that* … and nonintegral citations like *Studies have shown … (Xu, 2024)*. Additionally, there are also choices to be made about when to paraphrase, summarize, or quote from a source. Experienced academic writers also develop an understanding of which and how many sources to cite in a given situation and how to maintain their own voice when engaging with other sources (Wette, 2021). There is as well the challenge of learning to use documentation styles like APA or MLA consistently and accurately. Finally, and perhaps most importantly, students need to learn how source use relates to principles like copyright, intellectual property, and academic integrity—concepts that can be confusing, slippery, and context-dependent (e.g., Pecorari, 2016; Pennycook, 1996). None of these practices are a "natural" part of communication; instead, they must be learned and taught, often with some degree of trial and error.

There is often a tendency to view source use practices, especially plagiarism, as cultural, and though they may be to some extent, L2 writing scholars have also cautioned that such relationships are complex. For example, factors that might influence a writer's understanding of source use include their experience with different kinds of writing, their educational background, and their sense of authority over their texts (Pecorari, 2016). There is also the confounding issue that teachers and other gatekeepers themselves often differ in their understanding of ethical and effective source use, as well as their responses to perceived shortcomings (Pecorari & Shaw, 2012). Like so many aspects of academic writing, there are also important disciplinary variations in how sources are integrated into texts (Wette, 2021).

Given the complexity of source use, L2AW teachers should give careful consideration to how its use and instruction might be scaffolded and revisited throughout a course and larger curriculum. In planning L2AW instruction for source use, teachers might then consider questions like the following:

- What are the local institutional and program policies and practices for source use and academic integrity?
- What do students already know and what do they need to know?
- What (range of) disciplines are students preparing to write in?
- What kinds of genres will students write in?
- How familiar are students with textual conventions for source use (such as the use of reporting verb structure) and with documentation style systems?

Wette (2017) provides a very useful framework for identifying the types of practices that might be common for multilingual academic writers at different stages of experience. For instance, entry-level writers may make extensive use of paraphrasing and quotations, often citing one source at a time; intermediate-level writers may increasingly use multiple-source citations and may be able to use citations for a broad range of rhetorical functions. Given this general development, L2AW teachers can plan instruction that gradually adds complexity and allows students to build on what they know. (See, Wette, 2017, and Doolan & Fitzsimmons-Doolan, 2023, for extensive pedagogical examples.)

5.6 Technology Use

Technology is not an add-on in writing. Rather, it is embedded in the act of writing, which relies on various technological tools, whether they be pen and paper, stylus and digital tablet, laptop, mobile phone, or even virtual reality. Today, most academic writing is created in digital spaces, which bring with them a wide range of ever-evolving technologies. Learners may use computers or mobile devices to compose, collaborate, and revise; they may share their writing through digital spaces; they can edit their writing through apps like Grammarly or enhance the design of their texts or graphic design tools like Canva; and they can analyze and explore written texts aided by corpus technology. Quite simply, technology has altered both what we write and how we write.

Understandably, some writing teachers distrust the role of technology in the classroom or may feel that technology-enhanced elements of writing, such as the incorporation of multimodal resources, should be minimized in an L2 writing course. There are valid reasons for these concerns. Composing multimodal texts, for instance, can detract pedagogical attention away from important opportunities for language development (Manchón, 2017; Qu, 2017). AI too raises legitimate and serious ethical questions (Dakakni & Safa, 2023), not to mention concerns about writers becoming so reliant on such tools that they lose opportunities to develop their independent writing skills (Kubota, 2023; Warschauer et al., 2023). (See Section 6 for more discussion of AI in L2AW.)

Still, technology is so thoroughly integrated into writing, that it is not realistic or advisable to banish it from an L2AW classroom in most settings. In "real life," writers nearly always have access to spelling and grammar checkers, which are embedded in most apps with which we compose, from text messages to more robust word processing programs. Given the constant presence and availability of technology, especially in academic environments, it makes more sense for conversations to move toward *how* rather than *whether* it should be integrated.

Teaching Second Language Academic Writing 53

L2AW teaches are integrating technology in many ways, from digital multimodal composing (DMC) to use of assistive technology. Regarding DMC, we know that many educational settings are already moving to incorporate more DMC activities throughout the curriculum. For example, in a review of undergraduate syllabi at a US university, Lim and Polio (2020) identified a range of multimodal tasks assigned to students, including several that did not exist a few decades ago: professional web pages, video résumés, online discussion posts, and transforming an essay into a visual representation are all examples. L2AW classrooms, too, are starting to embrace the potential of DMC. In a review of sixty-eight research studies published from 2005 to 2022, Kessler (2024) identified at least twelve DMC writing activities in L2AW classrooms. These included (but weren't limited to) digital storytelling, research proposals, blogs or websites, multimodal reflections, infographics, and digital posters.

A common and valuable approach for implementing DMC in an L2AW classroom is by remixing or transforming a monomodal text into a multimodal text, typically for a new audience and in a new genre. For instance, students may first write a traditional monomodal argument essay and then transform it into a multimodal digital video (Cimasko & Shin, 2017), or they can adapt a research synthesis into a multimodal fact sheet (Tardy et al., 2020). Conversely, a digital multimodal text like an infographic can be used as a planning activity to scaffold a monomodal text (Maamuujav et al., 2020). This process of transformation can also heighten students' awareness of audience and genre, as they work to identify the affordances and limitations of different modalities for expressing meaning to different readers.

A second approach to integrating technology into an L2AW classroom is the use of writing-assistive technology such as editors, translators, feedback tools, and text generators (the latter of which is addressed in Section 6). Tech-driven editors and machine translators are now freely accessible for most multilingual academic writers, and research is just beginning to examine its impacts on writing processes. Lee (2020) found that when EFL writers used machine translation (MT) to correct their L2 writing (rather than to produce it), they viewed the tool positively and were able to see its potential as a writing strategy. Today, many students and teachers also have access to tools for automated writing evaluation (AWE), allowing them to receive feedback from a computer at any stage of the writing process (see Li et al., 2017, for a brief overview). Stapleton and Radia (2010) also highlight the potential for such assistive tools for building writers' autonomy and also reducing or even eliminating "some of the more tedious tasks of teachers and editors at all levels of writing ability" (p. 180). Nevertheless, research of assistive-technology tools generally finds that factors like language proficiency and digital literacy can play a role in the effectiveness—or perceptions of effectiveness—of such tools (e.g., Zhang, 2020; Zhang & Hyland, 2023) and students need explicit instructional guidance in order to use such tools effectively (e.g., Stapleton & Radia, 2010). Therefore, L2AW teachers should learn which technologies students are using or may use and then incorporate guidance in those tools in an ethical and critical way that also aids their writing development.

In determining appropriate roles for technology in their classes, L2AW teachers can weigh several concerns. First and foremost, what are the course goals or learning outcomes? That is, what do students need to learn? The answers to this question should guide teachers in making decisions about which technologies are needed and what role(s) they might play in instruction. For instance, if students need to learn to incorporate scholarly sources into their writing, they will need instruction in using databases and library search systems. They may also benefit from learning to use citation generators effectively. On the other hand, if students are learning to report on data-driven research, they may need to learn to create effective presentations of data, through tables, charts, graphs, or images.

Other important considerations for teachers include identifying the availability of technology for students (ensuring that access is equitable), the genres that students will produce in the course, and the functions that different technology tools will carry out in both learning and writing. Further, given the ubiquity of writing assistive technology, it is increasingly important for all academic writing classes to support students in developing ethical and effective uses of such tools. Finally, instruction can also help students develop strategies for and practice with writing *without* technology, as students may need to do in exam situations or other in-class writing contexts.

5.7 Creativity and Play

Creativity and play may not be the first attributes to come to mind for most people when thinking of academic writing. After all, academic writing has a (perhaps well earned) reputation for being dry and impersonal (Sword, 2012). Yet, creativity and play both have important potential for learning and therefore also can play a part in L2AW instruction.

Creativity here does not refer to "creative writing," which is often associated with personal narratives, poems, or fiction. Rather creativity is meant simply to reference opportunities for students' ownership, investment, and agency in their writing. Rather than simply following formulaic structures, student writers (*all* writers) tend to be more invested and engaged when they can bring aspects of their identities or goals into their writing in some way. Creativity can be incorporated into L2AW in low-stakes ways, such as through a playful title, the use of images or unique formatting, or inclusion of a unique bio-statement at the end of their assignment. These examples overlap with the notion of *play*; Warner (2024) characterizes the two concepts as "close semantic cousin[s]" (p. 107). In relation to language and writing, play can be considered "an activity in which people temporarily step outside of 'ordinary' practice (in this case, writing) and engage in activity that may involve different goals and/or roles, often involving rehearsal, experimentation, or ruleshifting with low risk" (Tardy, 2021, p. 3). Play is also a kind of disposition, "a stance vis-a-vis teaching and learning activities, as an orientation for engaging with designs in the language classroom, and as a relationship to social systems" (Warner, 2024, p. 107).

A body of research has outlined the benefits of play on language and literacy learning, including improved memorability of learning through a lowered affective state (Tarone, 2000), risk-taking and expanded language use through taking on new identities (Broner & Tarone, 2001), increased attention to form (Cazden, 1974), and expansion and change in a developing L2 system (Bell, 2012). More specifically in L2AW, play (and creative language use) offers writers opportunities for increased ownership over language, expression of different identities, expanded language and genre repertoires through risk-taking, and enhanced metacognitive and genre awareness (Tardy, 2021).

Including creativity and play here as an important pedagogical practice for L2AW is not to suggest that all teachers and classes should incorporate humor, creative writing, or resistance to academic norms. Instead, creativity and play offer a reminder that motivation, engagement, ownership, enjoyment, and reflection are critical pieces of language and writing development, and that they can be facilitated through creativity and play. Therefore, even in a high-stakes L2AW course focused on "serious" genres like academic publishing, teachers can surely find spaces for experimentation, risk-taking, and ownership, even if only in the *process* of writing.

Incorporating play into an L2AW can most easily occur through small, low-stakes tasks. For example, students can practice rewriting a particular text from different identity positions (expert, novice, cranky academic, etc.) to experiment with stance and identity features of language, or they can create a tweet or microblog post of the thesis from their in-progress paper (using the #TweetYourThesis hashtag) to try to distill the main point of their work; multimodal elements such as images, emojis, or hyperlinks can be added. Larger assignments can include imitating and then perhaps parodying a genre that students are studying (see Devitt, 2004; Swales, 1990). Students can also create hybrid genres, such as Hyon's (2017) example of a "chemical love story," in which students blend a research-based writing and romantic narrative or Devitt's (2004) assignment in which students stretch genre conventions to see how far they can bend a genre. Remixing is also a kind of genre play in which students creatively adapt a text they've written in one genre into a new one. For example, in a course we developed at my university, students transform their academic literature review into a fact sheet, blog post, or infographic, creating their new text in both their first language and in English (their L2). In a reflective letter, they explore the considerations they took into account while transforming the text into a new genre and in writing the new text in two languages, building their metalinguistic and genre awareness. Multimodal genres, such as digital stories or video essays, further offer opportunities for students to bring creativity to their writing while building repertoire of semiotic resources and genres (Hafner, 2014).

Activities like those described offer students a chance to break free from the normative, and often somewhat stifling, pressures of academic writing, while also having value for their development as writers. When considering what kind of role creativity and play might have in any individual L2AW classroom, teachers might ask:

- What are the primary goals of instruction?
- What kinds of writing and literacy practices are students engaged in?
- Where are the opportunities for low-stakes risk-taking?
- Where can students take ownership over their writing choices?
- Where can playful engagement with norms be incorporated and for what goals?
- In what ways can students bring their own experiences, identities, and agency to their writing in this class?

In describing a pedagogy of multiliteracy play, Warner (2024) advocates for a consideration of balancing *designs*, described as the development of students' repertoires of semiotic resources, and *desires*, "being in the flow of languaging activities, [dimensions] which do not fit tidily into thesis statements or even reflections, but make these same activities meaningful" (p. 183). In other words, L2AW teachers still need to help students develop facility with dominant language and writing norms, but they can do so perhaps most effectively by also finding ways to engage students and bringing joy to the experience of L2AW.

Teaching Second Language Academic Writing 57

> **Reflection**
>
> 1. Choose one of the practices described in this section and discuss with a partner or in a journal how this practice might be carried out differently when following different teaching approaches (as described in Section 4). For example, how might assessment be affected by a teacher's decision to implement process and genre approaches versus multiliteracies and translanguaging approaches?
> 2. Choose one of the practices from this section and consider how it might be implemented in two very different contexts. For example, consider how collaborative writing might be implemented in an online L2AW course for graduate students and in an in-person course for pre-university students. What are some ways that the context would influence how this practice is carried out?

6 Future Directions of Academic Writing

Academic writing is somewhat notorious for its slow pace of change and its adherence to conventions that have existed for decades or even longer. Yet, change is absolutely in the air, and not just in terms of scholarly understandings of academic writing or teaching approaches. There are also shifts in writing itself, including the semiotic resources used in today's academic writing, the genres that are used to communicate academic work, and the technologies that can have a big impact on composing processes. This final section explores two areas that are likely to have a significant impact on academic writing and the teaching of L2AW.

6.1 Emerging Academic Genres

Academic writing has always incorporated multiple modalities. Tables, charts, graphs, and images have long been common in the writing of many disciplines. In the predigital world, these modalities were largely produced in and shared through print. In most contexts today, however, the majority of academic writing lives only in the digital world, being produced, revised, and disseminated through gigabytes, screens, and pixels rather than A4 or letter-sized sheets of paper. As a result, the semiotic resources and modalities available to writers have expanded considerably. Even a basic word processor typically allows writers to insert still or animated images, equations, drawings, tables or charts, color, and video.

Unsurprisingly, this new multimodal potential has contributed to the evolution of many academic genres and even the emergence of new ones. For instance, academics are increasingly sharing their work with wider audiences via social media using genres like infographics, video explainers, TikToks, Tweet threads (tweetorials), video abstracts, graphic abstracts, research blogs, and three-minute thesis presentations. Though these emerging academic genres are all distinct, they share several common features:

- They are digital and multimodal, often blending alphabetic text with sound, images, and color.
- They are much shorter than traditional academic texts like research articles. They highlight key points and often omit details.
- They are shareable, either through specific social networking sites or more broadly on the Web. They can be linked to websites, email signature lines, or social media posts for wide distribution.
- Due to their short length and easy shareability, the texts tend to be produced for multiple audiences, including lay audiences or non-specialists.

Presently, emerging academic genres are being created, innovated, and gradually "typified" by researchers and scholars as they become more common (Luzón & Pérez-Llantada, 2022). It seems likely that such genres will also eventually find their way into the undergraduate curriculum. Indeed, there are many compelling reasons for undergraduate and even K–12 L2AW classrooms to engage students in these emerging academic genres. For example, exploration of emerging genres allows students to see the dynamic and variable nature of genres (Tardy et al., 2023). Additionally, the digital nature of most emerging academic genres can increase students' understanding of audience (Hafner, 2015), their motivation to engage readers (Hafner et al., 2013; Kim & Belcher, 2020), and their development of rhetorical flexibility as they write across genres and media (Caplan & Johns, 2019).

It is unlikely that emerging academic genres will displace the privileged positions of more traditional genres any time soon. Students will still need to learn and demonstrate an ability to write longer research-based texts that are largely comprised of written words, formal language, complex organization, conventions for source use, and disciplinary preferences for knowledge production. But traditional and new genres can coexist in L2AW instruction, and by exposing students to both, we can also raise their awareness of the complexity and richness of academic writing. Such adjustments will also require teachers to develop their own sets of skills in digital literacy, remixing, and use of design tools. As Bob Dylan famously wrote, "the times are a-changin'", and the world of L2AW is a pretty interesting place right now!

6.2 Artificial Intelligence

It would be an oversight to end this Element without discussing one of the most important changes affecting academic writing today, which is the development and wide scale availability of artificial intelligence (AI), especially in the form of large language models (LLMs) like ChatGPT. The release of ChatGPT in late 2022 had an almost immediate impact on academic writing. Through "prompting" (a user's specific guidance or requests to a chatbot), LLMs can produce texts that often look remarkably similar, at least at the surface level, to human writing. Teachers are still coming to grips with the implications of emerging AI technologies for writing and writing instruction, and we will most certainly continue to modify our understanding of the technology as it too evolves.

Early scholarship has identified both benefits and limitations of AI technology in assisting multilingual academic writers. On the positive side, such technology can help writers generate ideas, plan, and refine their texts; provide written corrective feedback to students at any time; and can grade work using an assignment's criteria to aid writers in self-assessment (Barrot, 2023). For example, a chatbot can be prompted to share possible research questions in a particular topic area, offering ideas that the writer can build on, reject, or adapt. Similarly, writers can share an assignment prompt, rubric, and draft with a chatbot and request feedback for revisions. While the feedback should not be used without very careful reflection, it can provide students one source of information to consider. As students are revising, teachers can ask them to summarize feedback they received from peers, their instructor, and possibly technology tools, then think critically about which areas they want to prioritize for revision. In this way, AI can offer one tool in students' writing development while the writer still retains agency and critical involvement in learning. In one study, Chinese graduate students writing in English as an additional language also reported that AI tools improved their writing efficiency and quality, and it facilitated their writing and thinking abilities (Zou & Huang, 2024). However, much more research is needed for us to properly understand the contributions and risks that such technology brings to multilingual writers' learning.

Limitations to AI technologies are also important to recognize—and there are many. At this point, AI-generated text still contains false information or "hallucinations," sometimes even generating references that do not exist. If students use such texts uncritically, they may spread misinformation through their writing (Zou & Huang, 2024). Crucially, ineffective use of AI may lead to learning loss, as students miss out on vital opportunities to develop as writers. As Warschauer et al. (2023) note, "Premature exposure to AI writing tools can inadvertently teach students to extensively and exclusively rely on these tools, robbing students of opportunities to develop the foundational writing skills that they will need to best use them in the future" (p. 3). Scholars have also pointed out that AI-generated texts tend to follow rigid structures (Barrot, 2023), promote normative rather than heterogeneous language use (Godwin-Jones, 2024), and lack emotion or authorial voice (Barrot, 2023; Zou & Huang, 2024).

As L2AW researchers and practitioners grapple with the implications of AI-assisted technologies, teaching students critical AI literacy is now essential. Such literacy includes an understanding of what AI is, how it does what it does, how its use complicates notions or originality and attribution, the power dynamics implicated in its use, related ethical concerns, and how to develop agency over AI (Godwin-Jones, 2024). It will take teachers time to develop resources for these many new areas of practice, but we can start by modeling effective uses and discussing with students what ineffective uses look like and how to avoid them.

Whatever an individual teacher's views are on AI, as well as their institutions or program's policies, the proverbial toothpaste is out of the tube. AI tools are most likely here to stay, and their impact on academic writing and L2AW classrooms is already substantial. For example, the larger academic publishing community is also reflecting on and exploring the role of AI in published writing and peer review, and the practices and policies developed in that area may eventually have an impact on academic writing for students as well. Further, some teachers are exploring how AI can support their own work, such as revising or creating assignment prompts, generating sample texts with variations to audience or purpose, supporting assessment, or gathering input for course design. There is a wide variation in terms of how effective or ethical such uses may or may not be, and there is also a full spectrum of perspectives on the extent to which AI technology is helpful, harmful, and/or unethical, and how it should be addressed in an L2AW classroom.

Fortunately, there is no shortage of current research into the role and impacts of AI on academic writing, including in multilingual contexts. In the next decade we are likely to see a cascade of new studies exploring AI technology in areas like composing processes, feedback, academic integrity, assessment, student and teacher attitudes, prompting AI tools, and developing critical AI literacies. Research is critical, but the perspectives and experiences of L2AW teachers are also essential to these developing conversations; indeed, the most significant innovations in L2AW are likely to come from teachers' own informed, reflective practice and their ongoing development of small-t theories that can guide their work. Amid the research attention that technology will most certainly gather, it will also be essential to study the unique and significant contributions of *humans* in teaching L2AW.

Reflection

1. If you are currently a writing teacher, reflect on writing assignments that you have recently included in your classes.

   a. To what extent do they include digital and multimodal elements? Is it sufficient?
   b. How has your teaching of academic genres changed (if at all) over the years? Do you include any emerging genres in your classroom instruction? Why or why not?

2. If you have not yet taught L2AW, reflect on your goals:

   a. To what extent do you feel that digital and multimodal features should be a part of the writing that students do in an L2AW classroom? Why?
   b. Should students write in emerging academic genres in an L2AW classroom, or should they focus on more traditional genres? Does your answer depend on the students' context? Explain.

3. What is your current stance regarding the use of AI-assisted writing technologies in the L2AW classroom, such as LLMs and automatic translators? Brainstorm some activities that could help students to build their critical AI literacy.

4. What guidance would you share with students in an L2AW classroom regarding the use of AI? Try to write out a policy or set of guidelines that you might share with your students. Consider how aspects of your teaching context (see Section 2) might influence these guidelines.

References

Allen, H. W. (2018). Redefining writing in the foreign language curriculum: Toward a design approach. *Foreign Language Annals, 51*(3), 513–532.

Atkinson, D. (2002). Toward a sociocognitive approach to second language acquisition. *The Modern Language Journal, 86*(4), 525–545.

Atkinson, D. (2004). Contrasting rhetorics/contrasting cultures: Why contrastive rhetoric needs a better conceptualization of culture. *Journal of English for Academic Purposes, 3*(4), 277–289.

Atkinson, D. (2010). Between theory with a big T and practice with a small p: Why theory matters. In T. Silva & P. K. Matsuda (Eds.), *Practicing theory in second language writing* (pp. 5–18). Parlor Press.

Atkinson, D. (2016). Second language writing and culture. In R. M. Manchón & P. K. Matsuda (Eds.), *Handbook of second and foreign language writing* (pp. 545–566). De Gruyter.

Atkinson, D., & Ramanathan, V. (1995). Cultures of writing: An ethnographic comparison of L1 and L2 university writing/language programs. *TESOL Quarterly, 29*(3), 539–568

Bakhtin, M. M. (1986). *Speech genres and other late essays*. University of Texas Press.

Barrot, J. S. (2023). Using ChatGPT for second language writing: Pitfalls and potentials. *Assessing Writing, 57*, 100745.

Bazerman, C. (1988). *Shaping written knowledge*. University of Wisconsin Press.

Bazerman, C., Little, J., Bethel, L. et al. (2005). *Reference guide to writing across the curriculum*. Parlor Press; The WAC Clearinghouse. https://wac.colostate.edu/books/referenceguides/bazerman-wac/.

Belcher, D. D. (2017). On becoming facilitators of multimodal composing and digital design. *Journal of Second Language Writing, 38*, 80–85.

Belcher, D. D. (2023). Digital genres: What they are, what they do, and why we need to better understand them. *English for Specific Purposes, 70*, 33–43.

Bell, N. (2012). Formulaic language, creativity, and language play in a second language. *Annual Review of Applied Linguistics, 32*, 189–205.

Benedict, R. (1934). *Patterns of culture*. Houghton-Mifflin.

Benesch, S. (2001). *Critical English for academic purposes: Theory, politics, and practice*. Routledge.

References 63

Biber, D., Gray, B., & Poonpon, K. (2011). Should we use characteristics of conversation to measure grammatical complexity in L2 writing development? *TESOL Quarterly, 45*(1), 5–35.

Bitchener, J., & Ferris, D. (2012). *Written corrective feedback in second language acquisition and writing.* Routledge.

Bizzell, P. (1992). *Academic discourse and critical consciousness.* University of Pittsburgh Press.

Blanton, L. (1994). Discourse, artifacts, and the Ozarks: Understanding academic literacy. *Journal of Second Language Writing, 3*, 1–16.

Blommaert, J., Collins, J., & Slembrouck, S. (2005). Spaces of multilingualism. *Language & Communication, 25*, 197–216.

Blum, S. D. (Ed.). (2020). *Ungrading: Why rating students undermines learning (and what to do instead).* West Virginia University Press.

Bocanegra-Valle, A. (2016). Needs analysis for curriculum design. In K. Hyland & P. Shaw (Eds.), *The Routledge handbook of English for academic purposes* (pp. 560–576). Routledge.

Broner, M. A., & Tarone, E. (2001). Is it fun? Language play in a fifth-grade Spanish immersion classroom. *The Modern Language Journal, 58*(4), 363–379.

Canagarajah, A. S. (2006). Toward a writing pedagogy of shuttling between languages: Learning from multilingual writers. *College English, 68*(6), 589–604.

Canagarajah, A. S. (Ed.). (2013). *Literacy as translingual practice: Between communities and classrooms.* Routledge.

Canagarajah, S. (2022). Language diversity in academic writing: Toward decolonizing scholarly publishing. *Journal of Multicultural Discourses, 17* (2), 107–128.

Canagarajah, S. (2024). Decolonizing academic writing pedagogies for multilingual students. *TESOL Quarterly, 58*(1), 280–306.

Caplan, N. A. (2022). The grammar choices that matter in academic writing. In E. Hinkel (Ed.), *Handbook of practical second language teaching and learning* (pp. 466–479). Routledge.

Caplan, N. A., & Cox, M. (2016). The state of graduate communication support: Results of an international survey. In S. Simpson, N. A. Caplan, M. Cox, & T. Phillips, (Eds.), *Supporting graduate student writers: Research, curriculum, & program design* (pp. 22–47). University of Michigan Press.

Caplan, N. A., & Farling, M. (2017). A dozen heads are better than one: Collaborative writing in genre-based pedagogy. *TESOL Journal, 8*(3), 564–581.

64 *References*

Caplan, N. A., & Johns, A. M. (Eds.). (2019). *Changing practices for the L2 writing classroom: Moving beyond the five-paragraph essay.* University of Michigan Press.

Casanave, C. P. (2005). *Writing games: Multicultural case studies of academic literacy practices in higher education.* Routledge.

Cazden, C. (1974). Play and metalinguistic awareness: One dimension of language experience. *The Urban Review, 7,* 28–39.

Cenoz, J. (2013). Defining multilingualism. *Annual Review of Applied Linguistics, 33,* 3–18.

Cenoz, J., & Gorter, D. (2021). *Pedagogical translanguaging.* Cambridge University Press.

Charles, M. (2012). English for academic purposes. In B. Paltridge & S. Starfield (Eds.), *The handbook of English for specific purposes* (pp. 137–153). Wiley-Blackwell.

Charles, M. (2018). Corpus tools for writing students. In D. Belcher & A. Hirvela (Eds.), *The TESOL Encyclopedia of English Language Teaching. Teaching Writing.* Wiley.

Cheng, A. (2008). Analyzing genre exemplars in preparation for writing: The case of an L2 graduate student in the ESP genre-based instructional framework of academic literacy. *Applied Linguistics, 29*(1), 50–71.

Cheng, A. (2018). *Genre and graduate-level research writing.* University of Michigan Press.

Conference on College Composition and Communication. (1974). Students' right to their own language. *College Composition and Communication, 25* (3), 1–32.

Cimasko, T., & Shin, D. S. (2017). Multimodal resemiotization and authorial agency in an L2 writing classroom. *Written Communication, 34*(4), 387–413.

Connor, U. (2011). *Intercultural rhetoric in the writing classroom.* University of Michigan Press.

Connor, U., Ene, E., & Traversa, A. (2016). Intercultural rhetoric. In K. Hyland & P. Shaw (Eds.), *The Routledge handbook of English for academic purposes* (pp. 270–282). Routledge.

Cook, V. J. (1992). Evidence for multicompetence. *Language Learning, 42*(4), 557–591.

Cook, V. (2012). Multicompetence. In C. Chapelle (Ed.), *The encyclopedia of applied linguistics.* Wiley.

Cope, B., & Kalantzis, M. (2015). *A pedagogy of multiliteracies: Learning by design.* Palgrave Macmillan.

Cope, B., & Kalantzis, M. (2023). Towards education justice: The multiliteracies project revisited. In G. C. Zapata, M. Kalantzis, & B. Cope (Eds.), *Multiliteracies in international educational contexts* (pp. 1–33). Routledge.

Corcoran, J. (2017). The potential and limitations of an intensive English for Research Publication Purposes course for Mexican scholars. In M. J. Curry & T. Lillis (Eds.), *Global academic publishing: Policies, perspectives and pedagogies* (pp. 233–248). Multilingual Matters.

Cotos, E., Huffman, S., & Link, S. (2020). Understanding graduate writers' interaction with and impact of the Research Writing Tutor during revision. *Journal of Writing Research*, *12*(1), 187–232.

Crusan, D. (2010). *Assessment in the second language writing classroom*. University of Michigan Press.

Crusan, D. (2024). Ungrading: Revolution or evolution? *Journal of Second Language Writing*, *66*, Article 101149.

Crusan, D., & Ruecker, T. (2022). *Linking assignments to assessments: A guide for teachers*. University of Michigan Press.

Cumming, A. (2016). Theoretical orientations to L2 writing. In R. M. Manchón & P. K. Matsuda (Eds.), *Handbook of second and foreign language writing* (pp. 65–88). De Gruyter.

Dakakni, D., & Safa, N. (2023). Artificial intelligence in the L2 classroom: Implications and challenges on ethics and equity in higher education: A 21st century Pandora's box. *Computers and Education: Artificial Intelligence*, *5*, 100179.

Devitt, A. J. (2004). *Writing genres*. SIU Press.

Doolan, S. M., & Fitzsimmons-Doolan, S. (2023). Scaffolding instruction for post-secondary L2 synthesis writing. In R. Wette (Ed.), *Teaching and learning source-based writing* (pp. 124–139). Routledge.

Eckstein, G., & Ferris, D. (2018). Comparing L1 and L2 texts and writers in first-year composition. *TESOL Quarterly*, *52*(1), 137–162.

Egbert, J., Larsson, T., & Biber, D. (2020). *Doing linguistics with a corpus: Methodological considerations for the everyday user*. Cambridge University Press.

Elabdali, R. (2021). Are two heads really better than one? A meta-analysis of the L2 learning benefits of collaborative writing. *Journal of Second Language Writing*, *52*, 100788.

Elbow, P. (1973). *Writing without teachers*. Oxford University Press.

Elbow, P. (1981). *Writing with power*. Oxford University Press.

English as a Lingua Franca in Academic Settings. (n.d.). ELFA corpus. www .helsinki.fi/en/researchgroups/english-as-a-lingua-franca-in-academic-set tings/research/elfa-corpus.

English as a Lingua Franca in Academic Settings. (n.d.). WRELFA corpus. https://www.helsinki.fi/en/researchgroups/english-as-a-lingua-franca-in-academic-settings/research/wrelfa-corpus.

Fernandez Dobao, A. (2012). Collaborative writing tasks in the L2 classroom: Comparing group, pair, and individual work. *Journal of Second Language Writing, 21*(1), 40–58.

Ferris, D. R. (2015). Inclusivity through community: Designing response systems for "mixed" academic writing courses. In M. Roberge, K. M. Losey, & M. Wald (Eds.), *Teaching US-educated multilingual writers: Pedagogical practices from and for the classroom* (pp. 11–46). University of Michigan Press.

Ferris, D. R., & Hedgcock, J. S. (2023). *Teaching L2 composition: Purpose, process, and practice* (4th ed.). Routledge.

Flores, N. (2020). From academic language to language architecture: Challenging raciolinguistic ideologies in research and practice. *Theory into Practice, 59*(1), 22–31.

Flower, L., & Hayes, J. R. (1981). A cognitive process theory of writing. *College Composition and Communication, 32*, 365–387.

Flowerdew, J. (2017). Corpus-based approaches to language description for specialized academic writing. *Language Teaching, 50*(1), 90–106.

Flowerdew, L. (2023). Corpora for EAP writing. In E. Csomay & R. R. Jablonkai (Eds.), *The Routledge handbook of corpora and English language teaching and learning* (pp. 234–247). Routledge.

Friginal, E. (2018). *Corpus linguistics for English teachers: Tools, online resources, and classroom activities*. Routledge.

Galloway, N., & Rose, H. (2015). *Introducing global Englishes*. Routledge.

Gee, J. P. (1989). Literacy, discourse, and linguistics: Introduction. *Journal of Education, 171*(1), 5–17.

Gentil, G. (2011). A biliteracy agenda for genre research. *Journal of Second Language Writing, 20*(1), 6–23.

Gentil, G. (2018). Multilingualism as a writing resource. In J. Liontas (Ed.), *TESOL encyclopedia of English language teaching*. Wiley.

Godwin-Jones, R. (2024). Distributed agency in second language learning and teaching through generative AI. *Language Learning & Technology, 28*(2), 5–31.

Hafner, C. A. (2014). Embedding digital literacies in English language teaching: Students' digital video projects as multimodal ensembles. *TESOL Quarterly, 48*(4), 655–685.

References

Hafner, C. A. (2015). Remix culture and English language teaching: The expression of learner voice in digital multimodal compositions. *TESOL Quarterly, 49*(3), 486–509.

Hafner, C. A., Chik, A., & Jones, R. H. (2013). Engaging with digital literacies in TESOL. *TESOL Quarterly, 47*(4), 812–815.

Halliday, M. A. K. (1978). *Language as social semiotic: The social interpretation of language and meaning.* Edward Arnold.

Hirvela, A., Hyland, K., & Manchón, R. M. (2016). Dimensions in L2 writing theory and research: Learning to write and writing to learn. In R. M. Manchón & P. K. Matsuda (Eds.), *Handbook of second and foreign language writing* (pp. 45–63). De Gruyter.

Holliday, A. (1994). *Appropriate methodology and social context.* Cambridge University Press.

Horner, B., & Trimbur, J. (2002). English only and US college composition. *College Composition and Communication, 53*, 594–630.

Horner, B., Lu, M. Z., Royster, J. J., & Trimbur, J. (2011). Language difference in writing: Toward a translingual approach. *College English, 73*(3), 303–321.

Hyland, K. (1999). Academic attribution: Citation and the construction of disciplinary knowledge. *Applied Linguistics, 20*(3), 341–367.

Hyland, K. (2005). Stance and engagement: A model of interaction in academic discourse. *Discourse Studies, 7*(2), 173–192.

Hyland, K. (2007). Genre pedagogy: Language, literacy, and L2 writing instruction. *Journal of Second Language Writing, 16*(3), 148–164.

Hyland, K. (2012). *Disciplinary identities: Individuality and community in academic discourse.* Cambridge University Press.

Hyland, K. (2016). General and specific EAP. In K. Hyland & P. Shaw (Eds.), *The Routledge handbook of English for academic purposes* (pp. 17–29). Routledge.

Hyland, K. (2019). *Second language writing.* Cambridge University Press.

Hyland, K., & Tse, P. (2004). Metadiscourse in academic writing: A reappraisal. *Applied Linguistics, 25*(2), 156–177.

Hynninen, N., & Kuteeva, M. (2017). "Good" and "acceptable" English in L2 research writing: Ideals and realities in history and computer science. *Journal of English for Academic Purposes, 30*, 53–65.

Hyon, S. (2017). *Introducing genre and English for specific purposes.* Routledge.

Ivanič, R. (1998). *Writing and identity: The discoursal construction of identity in academic writing.* John Benjamins Press.

Jewitt, C. (2006). *Technology, literacy and learning: A multimodal approach.* Routledge.

Jiang, L. G., & Hafner, C. (2024). Digital multimodal composing in L2 classrooms: A research agenda. *Language Teaching*, 1–19.

Johns, A. M. (1997). *Text, role and context: Developing academic literacies.* Cambridge University Press.

Johns, T. (1991). Should you be persuaded: Two samples of data-driven learning materials. In T. Johns & P. King (Eds.), *Classroom concordancing: ELR Journal 4* (pp. 1–16). Centre for English Language Studies, University of Birmingham

Johns, A. M. (2009). Situated invention and genres: Assisting generation 1.5 students in developing rhetorical flexibility. In M. Roberge, M. Siegal, & M. L. Harklau (Eds.), *Generation 1.5 in college composition* (pp. 213–230). Routledge.

Johns, A. M., Bawarshi, A., Coe, R. M. et al. (2006). Crossing the boundaries of genre studies: Commentaries by experts. *Journal of Second Language Writing, 15*(3), 234–249.

Kaplan, R. B. (1966). Cultural thought patterns in inter-cultural education. *Language Learning, 16*(1–2), 1–20.

Kachru, B. (1986). The power and politics of English. *World Englishes, 5*(2/3), 121–140.

Kalantzis, M., & Cope, B. (2010). The teacher as designer: Pedagogy in the new media age. *E-learning and Digital Media, 7*(3), 200–222.

Kalantzis, M., & Cope, B. (2024). *The knowledge processes.* Works & Days. June 14, 2024, https://newlearningonline.com/learning-by-design/the-knowledge-processes.

Kayı-Aydar, H. (2023). *Critical applied linguistics: An intersectional introduction.* Routledge.

Kern, R. (2000). *Literacy and language teaching.* Oxford University Press.

Kessler, M. (2020). Technology-mediated writing: Exploring incoming graduate students' L2 writing strategies with activity theory. *Computers and Composition, 55*, 102542.

Kessler, M. (2024). *Digital multimodal composing: Connecting theory, research and practice in second language acquisition.* Multilingual Matters.

Khadka, S. (2019). *Multiliteracies, emerging media, and college writing instruction.* Routledge.

Kibler, A. K. (2017). Becoming a "Mexican feminist": A minoritized bilingual's development of disciplinary identities through writing. *Journal of Second Language Writing, 38*, 26–41.

Kim, Y., & Belcher, D. (2020). Multimodal composing and traditional essays: Linguistic performance and learner perceptions. *RELC Journal, 51*(1), 86–100.

References

Kim, Y., Belcher, D., & Peyton, C. (2023). Comparing monomodal traditional writing and digital multimodal composing in EAP classrooms: Linguistic performance and writing development. *Journal of English for Academic Purposes, 64*, 101247.

King, K. A. (2000). Language ideologies and heritage language education. *International Journal of Bilingual Education and Bilingualism, 3*(3), 167–184.

Kress, G. (2017). What is a mode? In C. Jewitt (Ed.), *The Routledge handbook of multimodal analysis* (pp. 54–67). Routledge.

Kress, G. & Van Leeuwen, T. (1996). *Reading images: The grammar of visual design*. Routledge.

Kubota, R. (2002). Japanese identities in written communication: Politics and discourses. In R. T. Donahue (Ed.), *Exploring Japaneseness: On Japanese enactments of culture and consciousness* (pp. 293–315). Ablex.

Kubota, R. (2023). Another contradiction in AI-assisted second language writing. *Journal of Second Language Writing, 62*, 101069.

Kubota, R., & Lehner, A. (2004). Toward critical contrastive rhetoric. *Journal of Second Language Writing, 13*(1), 7–27.

Lasagabaster, D. (2022). *English-medium instruction in higher education*. Cambridge University Press.

Lea, M. R., & Street, B. V. (1998). Student writing in higher education: An academic literacies approach. *Studies in Higher Education, 23*(2), 157–172.

Lee, I. (2023). Problematising written corrective feedback: A global Englishes perspective. *Applied Linguistics, 44*(4), 791–796.

Lee, S. M. (2020). The impact of using machine translation on EFL students' writing. *Computer Assisted Language Learning, 33*(3), 157–175.

Lee, S. Y., Lo, Y. H. G., & Chin, T. C. (2019). Practicing multiliteracies to enhance EFL learners' meaning making process and language development: A multimodal problem-based approach. *Computer Assisted Language Learning, 34*(1–2), 66–91.

Leki, I., Cumming, A., & Silva, T. (2010). *A synthesis of research on second language writing in English*. Routledge.

Li, Z., Dursun, A., & Hegelheimer, V. (2017). Technology and L2 writing. In C. A. Chapelle & S. Sauro (Eds.), *The handbook of technology and second language teaching and learning* (pp. 77–92). Wiley.

Lillis, T., & Tuck, J. (2016). Academic literacies: A critical lens on writing and reading in the academy. In K. Hyland & P. Shaw (Eds.), *The Routledge handbook of English for academic purposes* (pp. 30–43). Routledge.

Lim, J., & Polio, C. (2020). Multimodal assignments in higher education: Implications for multimodal writing tasks for L2 writers. *Journal of Second Language Writing*, *47*, 100713.

Liu, P. H. E., & Tannacito, D. J. (2013). Resistance by L2 writers: The role of racial and language ideology in imagined community and identity investment. *Journal of Second Language Writing*, *22*(4), 355–373.

Losey, K. M., & Shuck, G. (Eds.) (2022). *Plurilingual pedagogies for multilingual writing classrooms*. Taylor & Francis.

Luzón, M. J., & Pérez-Llantada, C. (2022). *Digital genres in academic knowledge production and communication: Perspectives and practices*. De Gruyter.

Maamuujav, U., Krishnan, J., & Collins, P. (2020). The utility of infographics in L2 writing classes: A practical strategy to scaffold writing development. *TESOL Journal*, *11*(2), e484.

Macaro, E., Curle, S., Pun, J., An, J., & Dearden, J. (2018). A systematic review of English medium instruction in higher education. *Language Teaching*, *51*(1), 36–76.

Manchón, R. M. (2017). The potential impact of multimodal composing on language learning. *Journal of Second Language Writing*, *38*, 94–95.

Manchón, R. M., & Matsuda, P. K. (Eds.). (2016). *Handbook of second and foreign language writing* (Vol. 11). De Gruyter.

Manchón, R. M., Roca de Larios, J., & Murphy, L. (2007). A review of writing strategies: Focus on conceptualizations and impact of the first language. In A. Cohen & E. Macaro (Eds.), *Language learner strategies: Thirty years of research and practice* (pp. 229–250). Oxford University Press

Martin, J. R. (1992). Genre and literacy-modeling context in educational linguistics. *Annual Review of Applied Linguistics*, *13*, 141–172.

Matsuda, P. K. (1999). Composition studies and ESL writing: A disciplinary division of labor. *College Composition and Communication*, *50*(4), 699–721.

Matsuda, P. K. (2001). Voice in Japanese written discourse: Implications for second language writing. *Journal of Second Language Writing*, *10*(1), 35–53.

Matsuda, P. K. (2012). Let's face it: Language issues and the writing program administrator. *Writing Program Administration*, *36*(1), 141–164.

Matsuda, A., & Matsuda, P. K. (2010). World Englishes and the teaching of writing. *TESOL Quarterly*, *44*(2), 369–374.

Mauranen, A. (2012). *Exploring ELF: Academic English shaped by non-native speakers*. Cambridge University Press.

McGroarty, M. (2010). Language and ideologies. In N. E. Hornberger & S. L. McKay (Eds.), *Sociolinguistics and language education* (pp. 3–39). Multilingual Matters.

Michigan Corpus of Upper-level Student Papers. (2009). The Regents of the University of Michigan.

Migration Data Portal. (n.d.). International students. www.migrationdataportal.org/themes/international-students.

Miller, C. R. (1984). Genre as social action. *Quarterly Journal of Speech*, *70*(2), 151–167.

Mizumoto, A., & Eguchi, M. (2023). Exploring the potential of using an AI language model for automated essay scoring. *Research Methods in Applied Linguistics*, *2*(2), 100050.

Mizumoto, A., Shintani, N., Sasaki, M., & Teng, M. F. (2024). Testing the viability of ChatGPT as a companion in L2 writing accuracy assessment. *Research Methods in Applied Linguistics*, *3*(2), 100116.

Murphy, L., & Roca de Larios, J. (2010). Searching for words: One strategic use of the mother tongue by advanced Spanish EFL learners. *Journal of Second Language Writing*, *19*, 61–81.

Negretti, R., & McGrath, L. (2018). Scaffolding genre knowledge and meta-cognition: Insights from an L2 doctoral research writing course. *Journal of Second Language Writing*, *40*, 12–31.

Nesi, H., & Gardner, S. (2012). *Genres across the disciplines: Student writing in higher education*. Cambridge University Press.

The New London Group (1996). A pedagogy of multiliteracies: Designing social futures. *Harvard Educational Review*, *66*(1), 60–93.

Nowacek, R. S., Lorimer Leonard, R., & Rounsaville, A. (2024). *Writing knowledge transfer: Theory, research, pedagogy*. Parlor Press; The WAC Clearinghouse. https://wac.colostate.edu/books/referenceguides/transfer/.

Ortmeier-Hooper, C. (2008). English may be my second language, but I'm not "ESL." *College Composition & Communication*, *59*(3), 389–419.

Paesani, K.W., Allen, H.W., & Dupuy, B. (2015). *A multiliteracies framework for collegiate foreign language teaching*. Pearson.

Pecorari, D. (2016). Writing from sources, plagiarism and textual borrowing. In R. M. Manchón & P. K. Matsuda (Eds.), *Handbook of second and foreign language writing* (pp. 329–347). De Gruyter.

Pecorari, D., & Shaw, P. (2012). Types of student intertextuality and faculty attitudes. *Journal of Second Language Writing*, *21*(2), 149–164.

Peirce, B. (1995). Social identity, investment, and language learning. *TESOL Quarterly*, *29*, 9–31.

Pennycook, A. (1996). Borrowing others' words: Text, ownership, memory, and plagiarism. *TESOL Quarterly*, *30*(2), 201–230.

Pennycook, A. (1997). Vulgar pragmatism, critical pragmatism, and EAP. *English for Specific Purposes*, *16*(4), 253–269.

Polio, C. (2019). Keeping the language in second language writing classes. *Journal of Second Language Writing*, *46*, 100675.

Poole, R. (2016). A corpus-aided approach for the teaching and learning of rhetoric in an undergraduate composition course for L2 writers. *Journal of English for Academic Purposes*, *21*, 99–109.

Precht, K. (1998). A cross-cultural comparison of letters of recommendation. *English for Specific Purposes*, *17*(3), 241–265.

Qu, W. (2017). For L2 writers, it is always the problem of language. *Journal of Second Language Writing*, *38*, 92–93.

Reppen, R. (2010). *Using corpora in the language classroom*. Cambridge University Press.

Rinnert, C., & Kobayashi, H. (2016). Multicompetence and multilingual writing. In R. M. Manchón & P. K. Matsuda (Eds.), *Handbook of second and foreign language writing* (pp. 365–385). De Gruyter.

Roca de Larios, J., Nicolás-Conesa, F., & Coyle, Y. (2016). Focus on writers: Processes and strategies. In R. M. Manchón & P. K. Matsuda (Eds.), *Handbook of second and foreign language writing* (pp. 267–286). De Gruyter.

Roozen, K. (2016). Writing is a social and rhetorical activity. In L. Adler-Kassner & E. Wardle (Eds.), *Naming what we know: Threshold concepts of writing studies (Classroom ed.)* (pp. 17–19). University Press of Colorado.

Rozycki, W., & Johnson, N. H. (2013). Non-canonical grammar in Best Paper award winners in engineering. *English for Specific Purposes*, *32*(3), 157–169.

Rubin, D., & Williams-James, M. (1997). The impact of writer nationality on mainstream teachers' judgments of composition quality. *Journal of Second Language Writing*, *6*, 139–153.

Schoonen, R., Snellings, P., Stevenson, M., & van Gelderen, A. (2009). Towards a blueprint of the foreign language writer: The linguistic and cognitive demands of foreign language writing. In R. M. Manchón (Ed.), *Writing in foreign language contexts: Learning, teaching, and research* (pp. 77–101). Multilingual Matters.

Schreiber, B. R. (2020). Opening the door: Toward a framework for a translingual approach. In T. Silva & Z. Wang (Eds.), *Reconciling translingualism and second language writing* (pp. 225–234). Routledge.

References

Schreiber, B. R., Lee, E., Johnson, J. T., & Fahim, N. (Eds.). (2021). *Linguistic justice on campus: Pedagogy and advocacy for multilingual students*. Multilingual Matters.

Selvi, A. F., Galloway, N., & Rose, H. (2023). *Teaching English as an international language*. Cambridge University Press.

Séror, J., & Gentil, G. (2020). Cross-linguistic pedagogy and biliteracy in a bilingual university: Students' stances, practices, and ideologies. *Canadian Modern Language Review, 76*(4), 356–374.

Severino, C. (1993). The sociopolitical implications of response to second language writing. *Journal of Second Language Writing, 2*, 181–201.

Shapiro, S., & Leonard, R. L. (2023). Introduction to the special issue: Critical language awareness (CLA) as a lens for looking backward, outward, and forward in second language writing. *Journal of Second Language Writing, 60*, 101004.

Shin, D. S., & Cimasko, T. (2008). Multimodal composition in a college ESL class: New tools, traditional norms. *Computers and Composition, 25*(4), 376–395.

Shohamy, E. (2006). *Language policy: Hidden agendas and new approaches*. Routledge.

Silva, T., & Leki, I. (2004). Family matters: The influence of applied linguistics and composition studies on second language writing studies – Past, present, and future. *The Modern Language Journal, 88*(1), 1–13.

Silva, T., & Wang, Z. (Eds.). (2021). *Reconciling translingualism and second language writing*. Routledge.

Sims, M. L. (2023). Shifting perceptions of socially just writing assessment: Labor-based contract grading and multilingual writing instruction. *Assessing Writing, 57*, 100731.

Slinkard, J., & Gevers, J. (2020). Confronting internalized language ideologies in the writing classroom: Three pedagogical examples. *Composition Forum, 44*. https://compositionforum.com/issue/44/language-ideologies.php.

Smith, B. E., Pacheco, M. B., & Khorosheva, M. (2021). Emergent bilingual students and digital multimodal composition: A systematic review of research in secondary classrooms. *Reading Research Quarterly, 56*(1), 33–52.

Spolsky, B. (2004). *Language policy*. Cambridge University Press.

Staples, S., & Dilger, B. (2018). *Corpus and repository of writing* [Learner corpus articulated with repository]. https://crow.corporaproject.org.

Staples, S., & Reppen, R. (2016). Understanding first-year L2 writing: A lexico-grammatical analysis across L1s, genres, and language ratings. *Journal of Second Language Writing, 32*, 17–35.

74 *References*

Staples, S., Dang, A., & Wang, H. (2023). Learner corpora in corpus-informed instruction: Moving toward an asset-and genre-based model. *TESOL Quarterly*. Early view.

Stapleton, P., & Radia, P. (2010). Tech-era L2 writing: Towards a new kind of process. *ELT Journal*, *64*(2), 175–183.

Starfield, S. (2002). "I'm a second-language English speaker": Negotiating writer identity and authority in Sociology One. *Journal of Language, Identity and Education*, *1*, 121–140.

Stommel, J. (2020). How to ungrade. In S. D. Blum (Ed.), *Ungrading: Why rating students undermines learning (and what to do instead)* (pp. 25–41). West Virginia University Press.

Storch, N. (2013). *Collaborative writing in L2 classrooms*. Multilingual Matters.

Storch, N. (2016). Collaborative writing. In R. M. Manchón & P. K. Matsuda (Eds.), *Handbook of second and foreign language writing* (pp. 387–406). De Gruyter.

Sun, Y., Yang, K., & Silva, T. (2021). Multimodality in L2 writing: Intellectual roots and contemporary developments. In D.-S. Shin, T. Cimasko, & Y. Yi (Eds.), *Multimodal composing in K-16 ESL and EFL education: Multilingual perspectives* (pp. 3–16). Springer.

Swales, J. M. (1990). *Genre analysis*. Cambridge University Press.

Swales, J. M. (1997). English as Tyrannosaurus rex. *World Englishes*, *16*(3), 373–382.

Swales, J. M. (1998). *Other floors, other voices: A textography of a small university building*. University of Michigan Press.

Swales, J. M. (2004). *Research genres: Explorations and applications*. Cambridge University Press.

Swales, J. M., & Feak, C. B. (2020). *Academic writing for graduate students: Essential tasks and skills* (3rd ed.). University of Michigan Press.

Sword, H. (2012). *Stylish academic writing*. Harvard University Press.

Tan, X. (2023). Stories behind the scenes: L2 students' cognitive processes of multimodal composing and traditional writing. *Journal of Second Language Writing*, *59*, 100958.

Tardy, C. M. (2005). "It's like a story": Rhetorical knowledge development in advanced academic literacy. *Journal of English for Academic Purposes*, *4*(4), 325–338.

Tardy, C. M. (2011). Enacting and transforming local language policies. *College Composition and Communication*, *62*(4), 634–661.

Tardy, C. M. (2012). Voice construction, assessment, and extra-textual identity. *Research in the Teaching of English*, *47*(1), 64–99.

Tardy, C. M. (2016). *Beyond convention: Genre innovation in academic writing.* University of Michigan Press.

Tardy, C. M. (2021). The potential power of play in second language academic writing. *Journal of Second Language Writing, 53,* 100833.

Tardy, C. M. (2023). *Genre-based writing: What every ESL teacher needs to know.* University of Michigan Press.

Tardy, C. M., Caplan, N. A., & Johns, A. M. (2023). *Genre explained: Frequently asked questions (and answers) about genre-based instruction.* University of Michigan Press.

Tardy, C. M., Miller-Cochran, S. (2018). Administrative structures and support for international L2 writers: A heuristic for WPAs. In S. K Rose & I. Weiser (Eds.), *The internationalization of US writing programs* (pp. 60–76). University Press of Colorado.

Tardy, C. M., Sommer-Farias, B., & Gevers, J. (2020). Teaching and researching genre knowledge: Toward an enhanced theoretical framework. *Written Communication, 37*(3), 287–321.

Tarone, E. (2000). Getting serious about language play: Language play, interlanguage variation and second language acquisition. In B. Swierzbin, F. Morris, M. Anderson, C. Klee, & E. Tarone (Eds.), *Social and cognitive factors in SLA: Proceedings of the 1999 second language research forum* (pp. 31–54). Cascadilla Press.

UNESCO Institute for Statistics (UIS). (2024). *UIS.Stat.* https://data.uis.unesco.org/.

Valdés, G. (1992). Bilingual minorities and language issues in writing: Toward profession-wide responses to a new challenge. *Written Communication, 9,* 85–136.

Wardle, E. (2007). Understanding "transfer" from FYC: Preliminary results of a longitudinal study. *Writing Program Administration, 31,* 65–85.

Wardle, E. (2017). You can learn to write in general. In C. E. Ball & D. M. Loewe (Eds.), *Bad ideas about writing* (pp. 30–33). West Virginia University Libraries.

Warner, C. (2024). *Multiliteracy play: Designs and desires in the second language classroom.* Bloomsbury.

Warschauer, M., Tseng, W., Yim, S. et al. (2023). The affordances and contradictions of AI-generated text for writers of English as a second or foreign language. *Journal of Second Language Writing, 62,* 101071.

Weigle, S. C. (2002). *Assessing writing.* Cambridge University Press.

Weigle, S. C. (2016). Second language writing assessment. In R. M. Manchón & P. K. Matsuda (Eds.), *Handbook of second and foreign language writing* (pp. 473–493). De Gruyter.

Wette, R. (2017). L2 undergraduate students learning to write using sources: A trajectory of skill development. In J. Bitchener, N. Storch, & R. Wette (Eds.), *Teaching writing for academic purposes to multilingual students* (pp. 99–112). Routledge.

Wette, R. (2021). *Writing using sources for academic purposes theory, research and practice*. Taylor & Francis Group.

Wiley, T. G., & Lukes, M. (1996). English-only and standard English ideologies in the US. *TESOL Quarterly, 30*(3), 511–535.

Wu, X., & Lei, L. (2022). English as A Lingua Franca corpora and English language teaching. In E. Csomay & R. R. Jablonkai (Eds.), *The Routledge handbook of corpora and English language teaching and learning* (pp. 161–174). Routledge.

Yasuda, S. (2011). Genre-based tasks in foreign language writing: Developing writers' genre awareness, linguistic knowledge, and writing competence. *Journal of Second Language Writing, 20*(2), 111–133.

Yi, Y., Shin, D. S., & Cimasko, T. (2020). Multimodal composing in multilingual learning and teaching contexts. *Journal of Second Language Writing, 47*, 100717.

Yu, S., & Lee, I. (2016). Peer feedback in second language writing (2005–2014). *Language Teaching, 49*(4), 461–493.

Zhang, M., Gibbons, J., & Li, M. (2021). Computer-mediated collaborative writing in L2 classrooms: A systematic review. *Journal of Second Language Writing, 54*, 100854

Zhang, Z. V. (2020). Engaging with automated writing evaluation (AWE) feedback on L2 writing: Student perceptions and revisions. *Assessing Writing, 43*, 100439.

Zhang, Z., & Hyland, K. (2023). The role of digital literacy in student engagement with automated writing evaluation (AWE) feedback on second language writing. *Computer Assisted Language Learning*, 1–26.

Zhao, X. (2023). Leveraging artificial intelligence (AI) technology for English writing: Introducing wordtune as a digital writing assistant for EFL writers. *RELC Journal, 54*(3), 890–894.

Zou, M., & Huang, L. (2023). The impact of ChatGPT on L2 writing and expected responses: Voice from doctoral students. *Education and Information Technologies, 29*, 13201–13219.

Cambridge Elements ≡

Language Teaching

Heath Rose
University of Oxford

Heath Rose is Professor of Applied Linguistics at the University of Oxford and Deputy Director (People) of the Department of Education. Before moving into academia, Heath worked as a language teacher in Australia and Japan in both school and university contexts. He is author of numerous books, such as *Introducing Global Englishes, The Japanese Writing System, Data Collection Research Methods in Applied Linguistics,* and *Global Englishes for Language Teaching.*

Jim McKinley
University College London

Jim McKinley is Professor of Applied Linguistics at IOE Faculty of Education and Society, University College London. He has taught in higher education in the UK, Japan, Australia, and Uganda, as well as US schools. His research targets implications of globalization for L2 writing, language education, and higher education studies, particularly the teaching-research nexus and English medium instruction. Jim is co-author and co-editor of several books on research methods in applied linguistics. He is an Editor-in-Chief of the journal System.

Advisory Board

Gary Barkhuizen, *University of Auckland*
Marta Gonzalez-Lloret, *University of Hawaii*
Li Wei, *UCL Institute of Education*
Victoria Murphy, *University of Oxford*
Brian Paltridge, *University of Sydney*
Diane Pecorari, *Leeds University*
Christa Van der Walt, *Stellenbosch University*
Yongyan Zheng, *Fudan University*

About the Series

This Elements series aims to close the gap between researchers and practitioners by allying research with language teaching practices, in its exploration of research informed teaching, and teaching-informed research. The series builds upon a rich history of pedagogical research in its exploration of new insights within the field of language teaching.

Cambridge Elements ☰

Language Teaching

Elements in the Series

Task-Based Language Teaching
Daniel O. Jackson

Mediating Innovation through Language Teacher Education
Martin East

Teaching Young Multilingual Learners: Key Issues and New Insights
Luciana C. de Oliveira and Loren Jones

Teaching English as an International Language
Ali Fuad Selvi, Nicola Galloway and Heath Rose

Peer Assessment in Writing Instruction
Shulin Yu

Assessment for Language Teaching
Aek Phakiti and Constant Leung

Sociocultural Theory and Second Language Developmental Education
Matthew E. Poehner and James P. Lantolf

*Language Learning beyond English: Learner Motivation
in the Twenty-First Century*
Ursula Lanvers

Extensive Reading
Jing Zhou

Core Concepts in English for Specific Purposes
Helen Basturkmen

Willingness to Communicate in a Second Language
Jian E. Peng

Teaching Second Language Academic Writing
Christine M. Tardy

A full series listing is available at: www.cambridge.org/ELAT